FAVORITE BRAND NAME™

Best-Loved
RECIPES

Publications International, Ltd.

Favorite Brand Name Recipes at www.fbnr.com

Front cover photography by Proffitt Photography Ltd., Chicago.

Pictured on the front cover *(left to right):* Roasted Cornish Hen with Double Mushroom Stuffing *(pages 142, 109),* Green Beans with Toasted Pecans *(page 116)* and Very Cherry Pie *(page 218).*
Pictured on the back cover *(left to right):* Hash Brown Casserole *(page 14),* Sautéed Garlic Potatoes *(page 110)* and Chicken Tortilla Soup *(page 70).*

ISBN-13: 978-1-4127-2432-6
ISBN-10: 1-4127-2432-5

Library of Congress Control Number: 2006901040

Manufactured in China.

8 7 6 5 4 3 2 1

Microwave Cooking: Microwave ovens vary in wattage. Use the cooking times as guidelines and check for doneness before adding more time.

Preparation/Cooking Times: Preparation times are based on the approximate amount of time required to assemble the recipe before cooking, baking, chilling or serving. These times include preparation steps such as measuring, chopping and mixing. The fact that some preparations and cooking can be done simultaneously is taken into account. Preparation of optional ingredients and serving suggestions is not included.

contents

Hash Brown Casserole *(page 14)*

Green's "Dare to Dip 'em" Donut *(page 12)*

Start your day off
right with these
palate-pleasing
coffeecakes, egg
dishes, oatmeal,
muffins and more.

rise & shine

Apple Crumb Coffeecake *(page 32)*

Summer Sausage 'n' Egg Wedges

4 eggs, beaten
⅓ cup milk
¼ cup all-purpose flour
½ teaspoon baking powder
⅛ teaspoon garlic powder
2½ cups (10 ounces) shredded Cheddar or mozzarella cheese, divided
1½ cups diced HILLSHIRE FARM® Summer Sausage
1 cup cream-style cottage cheese with chives

Preheat oven to 375°F.

Combine eggs, milk, flour, baking powder and garlic powder in medium bowl; beat until combined. Stir in 2 cups Cheddar cheese, Summer Sausage and cottage cheese. Pour into greased 9-inch pie plate. Bake, uncovered, 25 to 30 minutes or until golden and knife inserted into center comes out clean. To serve, cut into 6 wedges. Sprinkle wedges with remaining ½ cup Cheddar cheese.   *Makes 6 servings*

tip:

There are six size classifications for eggs: jumbo, extra large, large, medium, small and peewee. The classification is determined by the minimum weight allowed per dozen. Any size egg can be used for scrambling, frying, poaching, etc. However, most recipes that call for eggs were developed using large eggs. Unless otherwise specified in the recipe, always use large eggs.

Summer Sausage 'n' Egg Wedge

Eggs Santa Fe

2 eggs

½ cup GUILTLESS GOURMET® Black Bean Dip (Spicy or Mild)

¼ cup GUILTLESS GOURMET® Southwestern Grill Salsa

1 ounce (about 20) GUILTLESS GOURMET® Unsalted Baked Tortilla Chips

2 tablespoons low fat sour cream

1 teaspoon chopped fresh cilantro

Fresh cilantro sprigs (optional)

To poach eggs, bring water to a boil in small skillet over high heat; reduce heat to medium-low and maintain a simmer. Gently break eggs into water, being careful not to break yolks. Cover and simmer 5 minutes or until desired firmness.

Meanwhile, place bean dip in small microwave-safe bowl. Microwave bean dip on HIGH (100% power) 2 to 3 minutes. To serve, spread ¼ cup warm bean dip in center of serving plate; top with 1 poached egg and 2 tablespoons salsa. Arrange 10 tortilla chips around egg. Dollop with 1 tablespoon sour cream and sprinkle with ½ teaspoon chopped cilantro. Repeat with remaining ingredients. Garnish with cilantro sprigs, if desired. *Makes 2 servings*

Golden Apple Oatmeal

½ cup diced Washington Golden Delicious apple

⅓ cup apple juice

⅓ cup water

¼ teaspoon salt (optional)

⅛ teaspoon ground cinnamon

⅛ teaspoon ground nutmeg

⅓ cup uncooked quick-cooking rolled oats

In small pot, combine apple, juice, water, salt, if desired, cinnamon and nutmeg; heat to a boil. Stir in oats and cook 1 minute. Cover and let stand 2 minutes before serving.

Makes 2 (½-cup) servings

Favorite recipe from **Washington Apple Commission**

Egg Santa Fe

Bacon-Cheese Muffins

½ **pound bacon (10 to 12 slices)**
   Vegetable oil
 1 **egg, beaten**
¾ **cup milk**
1¾ **cups all-purpose flour**
¼ **cup sugar**
 1 **tablespoon baking powder**
 1 **cup (4 ounces) shredded Wisconsin Cheddar cheese**
½ **cup crunchy nutlike cereal nuggets**

Preheat oven to 400°F. In large skillet, cook bacon over medium-high heat until crisp. Drain, reserving drippings. If necessary, add oil to drippings to measure ⅓ cup. In small bowl, combine dripping mixture, egg and milk; set aside. Crumble bacon; set aside.

In large bowl, combine flour, sugar and baking powder. Make well in center. Add egg mixture all at once to flour mixture, stirring just until moistened. Batter should be lumpy. Fold in bacon, cheese and cereal. Spoon into greased or paper-lined 2½-inch muffin cups, filling about ¾ full. Bake 15 to 20 minutes or until golden. Remove from pan. Cool on wire rack.

Makes 12 muffins

Favorite recipe from **Wisconsin Milk Marketing Board**

Bacon-Cheese Muffins

Green's "Dare to Dip 'em" Donuts

¼ cup (½ stick) butter, softened
⅓ cup granulated sugar
1 egg
½ teaspoon vanilla extract
1¾ cups all-purpose flour, divided
1 teaspoon baking powder
1 teaspoon ground cinnamon
½ teaspoon baking soda
¼ teaspoon salt
⅓ cup buttermilk
  Vegetable oil for frying
2 tablespoons powdered sugar
  Chocolate Glaze (page 13)
½ cup "M&M's"® Chocolate Mini Baking Bits

In large bowl cream butter and granulated sugar until light and fluffy; beat in egg and vanilla. In medium bowl combine flour, baking powder, cinnamon, baking soda and salt. Alternately add one-third flour mixture and half of buttermilk to creamed mixture, ending with flour mixture. Wrap and refrigerate dough 2 to 3 hours. On lightly floured surface roll dough to ½-inch thickness. Cut into rings using 2½-inch cookie cutter; reserve donut holes. Heat about 2 inches oil to 375°F in deep-fat fryer or deep saucepan. Fry donuts, 2 to 3 at a time, about 30 seconds on each side or until golden brown. Fry donut holes 10 to 15 seconds per side or until golden brown. Remove from oil; drain on paper towels. Cool completely. Place donut holes and powdered sugar in large plastic food storage bag; seal bag. Shake bag until donut holes are evenly coated. Prepare Chocolate Glaze. Dip donuts into glaze; decorate with "M&M's"® Chocolate Mini Baking Bits. Store in tightly covered container.

Makes 12 donuts and 12 donut holes

Chocolate Glaze

   1 cup powdered sugar

   1 tablespoon plus 1 teaspoon unsweetened cocoa powder

   1 tablespoon plus 1 teaspoon water

   ¾ teaspoon vanilla extract

In medium bowl combine powdered sugar and cocoa powder. Stir in water and vanilla; mix well.

Raisin Scones

Prep Time: 25 minutes
Bake Time: 15 minutes

   2¼ cups all-purpose flour

   ⅓ cup sugar

   1 tablespoon grated orange peel

   2¼ teaspoons baking powder

   ½ teaspoon baking soda

   ¼ teaspoon salt

   ½ cup (1 stick) margarine

   1 cup DOLE® Seedless Raisins

   ½ cup nonfat milk or plain yogurt

   1 teaspoon vanilla extract

• Combine flour, sugar, orange peel, baking powder, baking soda and salt.

• Cut in margarine, using two knives or pastry blender, until mixture resembles coarse crumbs.

• Stir in raisins. Combine milk and vanilla. Stir into mixture.

• Form dough into two balls. Pat one ball, on floured board, into 6-inch circle (½-inch thick). Cut into 6 wedges. Repeat with remaining dough. Place on baking sheet sprayed with cooking spray. Bake at 400°F 15 minutes. Cool on rack.   *Makes 12 servings*

Hash Brown Casserole

6 eggs, well beaten

1 can (12 fluid ounces) NESTLÉ® CARNATION® Evaporated Milk

1 teaspoon salt

½ teaspoon ground black pepper

1 package (30 ounces) frozen shredded hash brown potatoes

2 cups (8 ounces) shredded cheddar cheese

1 medium onion, chopped

1 small green bell pepper, chopped

1 cup diced ham (optional)

PREHEAT oven to 350°F. Grease 13×9-inch baking dish.

COMBINE eggs, evaporated milk, salt and black pepper in large bowl. Add potatoes, cheese, onion, bell pepper and ham, if desired; mix well. Pour mixture into prepared baking dish.

BAKE for 60 to 65 minutes or until set.   *Makes 12 servings*

tip:

The distinctive flavors of hams are produced by the pigs' diet—peanuts, acorns, apples, corn or peaches—and the type of wood over which they are smoked—apple, hictory or oak.

Hash Brown Casserole

Homemade Cinnamon Rolls

4¼ to 4¾ cups all-purpose flour, divided
1 package quick-rising active dry yeast
1¼ cups plus 4 to 5 teaspoons milk, divided
¼ cup granulated sugar
¼ cup (½ stick) plus 6 tablespoons butter, softened, divided
2 teaspoons WATKINS® Vanilla, divided
5 teaspoons WATKINS® Ground Cinnamon, divided
1 teaspoon salt
2 eggs
½ cup packed brown sugar
1 cup powdered sugar

Combine 1½ cups flour and yeast in large bowl. Heat 1¼ cups milk, granulated sugar, ¼ cup butter, 1 teaspoon vanilla, 1 teaspoon cinnamon and salt just until mixture is warm (120° to 130°F), stirring constantly. Add to flour mixture with eggs; beat with electric mixer at low speed for 30 seconds, scraping side of bowl frequently. Beat at high speed for 3 minutes.

Stir in as much remaining flour as possible with spoon (dough will be soft). Knead in enough remaining flour to form moderately soft dough, 3 to 5 minutes total. Shape dough into a ball; place in lightly greased bowl, turning once. Cover and let rise in warm place for about 1 to 1½ hours until doubled in size. Punch down dough and divide in half. Place each half on lightly floured surface and smooth into a ball. Cover and let rest 10 minutes.

Preheat oven to 350°F. Grease 13×9-inch baking pan. Roll half of dough into 12×8-inch rectangle on lightly floured surface. Spread with 3 tablespoons butter. Combine brown sugar and remaining 4 teaspoons cinnamon; sprinkle half of mixture over rectangle. Roll up dough from short side; seal edges by brushing with water. Repeat with remaining dough. Slice one roll into 8 pieces and other into 7 pieces. Arrange slices cut sides up in prepared pan. Cover and let rise for about 30 minutes or until nearly doubled.

Bake for 25 to 40 minutes or until light brown. Immediately invert rolls onto wire rack, then invert again. Cool slightly on wire rack. Combine powdered sugar, remaining 4 teaspoons milk and 1 teaspoon vanilla in small bowl until smooth; drizzle glaze over rolls. Serve warm or store in airtight container.

Makes 15 rolls

Homemade Cinnamon Rolls

French Toast

2 eggs, lightly beaten
½ cup milk
½ teaspoon WATKINS® Vanilla
¼ teaspoon salt
6 slices day-old bread
1 tablespoon butter

Combine eggs, milk, vanilla and salt in shallow bowl; mix well. Dip bread slices in egg mixture. Melt butter in large skillet; cook bread until golden brown on both sides. Serve hot with maple syrup, powdered sugar or tart jelly. *Makes 3 servings*

Down-Home Sausage Gravy

1 package (16 ounces) fresh breakfast sausage
2 tablespoons finely chopped onion
6 tablespoons all-purpose flour
2 cans (12 fluid ounces *each*) NESTLÉ® CARNATION® Evaporated Milk
1 cup water
¼ teaspoon salt
   Hot pepper sauce to taste
   Hot biscuits

COMBINE sausage and onion in large skillet. Cook over medium-low heat, stirring occasionally, until sausage is no longer pink. Stir in flour; mix well. Stir in evaporated milk, water, salt and hot pepper sauce. Cook, stirring occasionally, until mixture comes to a boil. Cook for 1 to 2 minutes.

SERVE immediately over biscuits. *Makes 8 to 10 servings*

Raisin-Streusel Coffeecake

1½ cups all-purpose flour

 2 teaspoons baking powder

¼ teaspoon baking soda

¼ teaspoon salt

¾ cup granulated sugar

 2 tablespoons margarine, softened

¾ cup nonfat sour cream

 1 egg

 1 teaspoon vanilla extract

½ cup MOTT'S® Chunky Apple Sauce

⅓ cup firmly packed light brown sugar

¼ cup raisins

 2 tablespoons crunchy nut-like cereal nuggets

1. Preheat oven to 350°F. Spray 9-inch round cake pan with nonstick cooking spray.

2. In small bowl, combine flour, baking powder, baking soda and salt.

3. In large bowl, beat granulated sugar and margarine with electric mixer at medium speed until blended. Whisk in sour cream, egg and vanilla. Gently mix in apple sauce.

4. Add flour mixture to apple sauce mixture; stir until well blended. Pour batter into prepared pan.

5. In small bowl, combine brown sugar, raisins and cereal. Sprinkle over batter.

6. Bake 50 minutes or until toothpick inserted into center comes out clean. Cool 15 minutes on wire rack. Serve warm or cool completely. Cut into 14 wedges. *Makes 14 servings*

Easy Morning Strata

1 pound BOB EVANS® Original Recipe Roll Sausage

8 eggs

10 slices bread, cut into cubes (about 10 cups)

3 cups milk

2 cups (8 ounces) shredded Cheddar cheese

2 cups (8 ounces) sliced fresh mushrooms

1 (10-ounce) package frozen cut asparagus, thawed and drained

2 tablespoons butter or margarine, melted

2 tablespoons all-purpose flour

1 tablespoon dry mustard

2 teaspoons dried basil leaves

1 teaspoon salt

Crumble sausage into large skillet. Cook over medium heat until browned, stirring occasionally. Drain off any drippings. Whisk eggs in large bowl. Add sausage and remaining ingredients; mix well. Spoon into greased 13×9-inch baking dish. Cover; refrigerate 8 hours or overnight. Preheat oven to 350°F. Bake 60 to 70 minutes or until knife inserted near center comes out clean. Let stand 5 minutes before cutting into squares; serve hot. Refrigerate leftovers. *Makes 10 to 12 servings*

Easy Morning Strata

Toll House® Mini Morsel Pancakes

2½ cups all-purpose flour

1 cup (6 ounces) NESTLÉ® TOLL HOUSE® Semi-Sweet Chocolate Mini Morsels

1 tablespoon baking powder

½ teaspoon salt

1¾ cups milk

2 eggs

⅓ cup vegetable oil

⅓ cup packed brown sugar

Powdered sugar

Fresh sliced strawberries

Maple syrup

COMBINE flour, morsels, baking powder and salt in large bowl. Combine milk, eggs, vegetable oil and brown sugar in medium bowl; add to flour mixture. Stir just until moistened (batter may be lumpy).

HEAT griddle or skillet over medium heat; brush lightly with vegetable oil. Pour ¼ *cup* of batter onto hot griddle; cook until bubbles begin to burst. Turn; continue to cook for about 1 minute longer or until golden. Repeat with *remaining* batter.

SPRINKLE with powdered sugar; top with strawberries. Serve with maple syrup.

Makes about 18 pancakes

Toll House® Mini Morsel Pancakes

Pecan Sticky Buns

Prep Time: 30 minutes plus chilling
Bake Time: 28 to 30 minutes

DOUGH*

4½ to 5½ cups all-purpose flour, divided
½ cup granulated sugar
1½ teaspoons salt
2 packages active dry yeast
¾ cup warm milk (105° to 115°F)
½ cup warm water (105° to 115°F)
¼ cup (½ stick) margarine or butter, softened
2 eggs

GLAZE

½ cup KARO® Light or Dark Corn Syrup
½ cup packed light brown sugar
¼ cup (½ stick) margarine or butter
1 cup pecans, coarsely chopped

FILLING

½ cup firmly packed light brown sugar
1 teaspoon ground cinnamon
2 tablespoons margarine or butter, melted

To use frozen bread dough, omit ingredients for dough. Thaw two 1-pound loaves frozen bread dough in refrigerator overnight. In step 3, press loaves together and roll to a 20×12-inch rectangle; complete as recipe directs.

continued on page 26

Pecan Sticky Buns

Pecan Sticky Buns, continued

1. For Dough: In large bowl combine 2 cups flour, granulated sugar, salt and yeast. Stir in milk, water and softened margarine until blended. Stir in eggs and enough additional flour (about 2 cups) to make a soft dough. Knead on floured surface until smooth and elastic, about 8 minutes. Cover dough and let rest on floured surface 10 minutes.

2. For Glaze: Meanwhile, in small saucepan over low heat stir corn syrup, brown sugar and margarine until smooth. Pour into 13×9×2-inch baking pan. Sprinkle with pecans; set aside.

3. For Filling: Combine brown sugar and cinnamon; set aside. Roll dough to a 20×12-inch rectangle. Brush dough with 2 tablespoons melted margarine; sprinkle with brown sugar mixture. Starting from a long side, roll up jelly-roll fashion. Pinch seam to seal. Cut into 15 slices. Place cut side up in prepared pan. Cover tightly. Refrigerate 2 to 24 hours.

4. To bake, preheat oven to 375°F. Remove pan from refrigerator. Uncover pan and let stand at room temperature 10 minutes. Bake 28 to 30 minutes or until tops are browned. Invert onto serving tray. Serve warm or cool completely. *Makes 15 rolls*

Country Ham Omelets

  2 tablespoons butter or margarine
  3 slices HILLSHIRE FARM® Ham, chopped
  ½ cup finely chopped potato
  ¼ cup chopped green bell pepper
  ¼ cup chopped onion
  ½ cup sliced fresh mushrooms
  8 to 12 eggs, beaten
  ½ cup (2 ounces) shredded sharp Cheddar cheese

Melt butter in medium skillet over medium heat; sauté Ham, potato, bell pepper and onion 3 to 4 minutes. Add mushrooms; stir and heat through.

Prepare four 2- or 3-egg omelets. Fill each with 2 tablespoons cheese and ¼ cup ham mixture. Use remaining ham mixture as omelet topping. *Makes 4 servings*

Homemade Granola

   2 cups uncooked old-fashioned oats
   1 cup flaked coconut
   ½ cup sunflower seeds
   ¼ cup (½ stick) butter
   ¼ cup brown sugar
   ¼ cup honey
  1½ teaspoons WATKINS® Vanilla
   1 teaspoon WATKINS® Ground Cinnamon
   ¼ teaspoon WATKINS® Nutmeg
   ½ cup toasted wheat germ
   1 cup raisins
   ½ cup dried fruit bits (apricots, raisins, apples)

Preheat oven to 300°F. Combine oats, coconut and sunflower seeds on large baking sheet with sides; mix well and spread out evenly. Bake for 20 minutes, stirring several times. Meanwhile, combine butter, brown sugar, honey, vanilla, cinnamon and nutmeg in small saucepan. Cook, stirring constantly, over medium heat until butter is melted and mixture is well blended. Remove from heat.

Remove baking sheet from oven; increase oven temperature to 350°F. Add wheat germ to oat mixture on baking sheet. Pour warm honey mixture over oat mixture; stir with spoon or spatula until thoroughly coated. Return to oven and bake for 5 minutes. Stir in raisins and dried fruit bits; mix well and spread out evenly. Return pan to oven and bake for 5 to 10 minutes or until golden brown. Pour granola onto large piece of foil; cool completely. Store in an airtight container for up to 2 weeks.   *Makes 6 cups (12 servings)*

Cranberry Sunshine Muffins

1½ cups all-purpose flour

½ cup SPLENDA® No Calorie Sweetener, Granular

2 teaspoons baking powder

1 teaspoon baking soda

½ teaspoon ground cinnamon

1 cup chopped fresh or frozen cranberries

¼ cup chopped walnuts

½ cup orange juice

¼ cup nonfat sour cream

1 egg or equivalent in egg substitute

1 tablespoon plus 1 teaspoon reduced-calorie margarine

1. Preheat oven to 375°F. Spray 8 muffin pan cups with butter-flavored cooking spray or line with paper liners.

2. In large bowl, combine flour, SPLENDA®, baking powder, baking soda and cinnamon. Stir in cranberries and walnuts.

3. In small bowl, combine orange juice, sour cream, egg and margarine. Add liquid mixture to dry mixture. Stir gently just to combine. Evenly spoon batter into prepared muffin cups.

4. Bake for 15 to 20 minutes or until toothpick inserted into centers come out clean. Cool in pan on wire rack for 5 minutes. Remove muffins from pan and continue cooling on wire rack.

Makes 8 servings

tip:

Fill unused muffin cups with water. It protects the muffin pan and ensures even baking.

Cranberry Sunshine Muffins

Brunch Sandwiches

Preparation Time: 5 minutes
Cooking Time: 10 minutes

> 4 English muffins, split, lightly toasted
> 8 thin slices CURE 81® ham
> 8 teaspoons Dijon mustard
> 8 eggs, fried or poached
> 8 slices SARGENTO® Deli Style Sliced Swiss Cheese

1. Top each muffin half with a slice of ham, folding to fit. Spread mustard lightly over ham; top with an egg and one slice cheese.

2. Transfer to foil-lined baking sheet. Broil 4 to 5 inches from heat source until cheese is melted and sandwiches are hot, 2 to 3 minutes.   *Makes 4 servings*

Spiced Apple Toast

> 1 tablespoon margarine
> 2 all-purpose apples, unpeeled, cored and thinly sliced
> ⅓ cup orange juice
> 4 teaspoons packed brown sugar
> ½ teaspoon ground cinnamon
> 4 slices whole wheat bread, toasted
> 2 teaspoons granulated sugar

Preheat oven to 450°F. Melt margarine in medium nonstick skillet. Add apples, orange juice, brown sugar and cinnamon; cook over medium-high heat about 4 minutes or until apples are tender, stirring occasionally. Drain; reserve cooking liquid. Cool apples 2 to 3 minutes. Place toast on lightly buttered baking sheet. Arrange apples, overlapping slices, in spiral design. Sprinkle ½ teaspoon granulated sugar over each slice. Bake 4 to 5 minutes or until bread is crisp. Drizzle reserved liquid over slices; serve immediately.   *Makes 4 servings*

Favorite recipe from **The Sugar Association, Inc.**

Brunch Sandwiches

Apple Crumb Coffeecake

2¼ cups all-purpose flour, divided
½ cup sugar
1 envelope FLEISCHMANN'S® RapidRise™ Yeast
½ teaspoon salt
¼ cup water
¼ cup milk
⅓ cup butter or margarine
2 eggs
2 cooking apples, cored and sliced
Crumb Topping (recipe follows)

In large bowl, combine 1 cup flour, sugar, undissolved yeast and salt. Heat water, milk and butter until very warm (120° to 130°F). Gradually add to dry ingredients. Beat 2 minutes at medium speed of electric mixer, scraping bowl occasionally. Add eggs and ½ cup flour. Beat 2 minutes at high speed, scraping bowl occasionally. Stir in remaining ¾ cup flour to make stiff batter. Spread evenly in greased 9-inch square pan. Arrange apple slices evenly over batter. Sprinkle Crumb Topping over apples. Cover; let rise in warm, draft-free place until doubled in size, about 1 hour.

Bake at 375°F for 35 to 40 minutes or until done. Cool in pan 10 minutes. Remove from pan; cool on wire rack. *Makes 1 (9-inch) cake*

Crumb Topping: Combine ⅓ cup sugar, ¼ cup all-purpose flour, 1 teaspoon ground cinnamon and 3 tablespoons cold butter or margarine. Use a pastry blender to mix all ingredients until coarse crumbs form.

Banana Nut Bread

2 ripe, large DOLE® Bananas
⅔ cup sugar
⅓ cup butter, softened
2 eggs
2 cups all-purpose flour
2 teaspoons baking powder
½ teaspoon baking soda
½ cup buttermilk
¾ cup chopped nuts

• Purée bananas in blender to measure 1¼ cups. Cream sugar and butter until light and fluffy. Beat in bananas and eggs. Combine flour, baking powder and baking soda. Add dry ingredients to banana mixture alternately in thirds with buttermilk, blending well after each addition. Stir in nuts.

• Pour into greased 9×5-inch loaf pan. Bake at 350°F 50 to 60 minutes or until wooden toothpick inserted in center comes out clean. Cool in pan on wire rack 10 minutes. Remove from pan and cool completely.   *Makes 1 loaf*

Shortcut "Sourdough" Corn Bread *(page 52)*

Braided Sandwich Ring *(page 58)*

bountiful breads

Fill your bread basket with plenty of warm, savory yeast breads straight from the oven or bread machine.

Herb Corn Bread *(page 36)*

Herb Corn Bread

1-POUND LOAF

- ½ cup water
- ½ cup evaporated milk
- 2 tablespoons vegetable oil
- Pinch dried sweet marjoram
- Pinch ground ginger
- ¾ teaspoon celery seed
- ¾ teaspoon dried sage
- 1 teaspoon salt
- 2 tablespoons sugar
- ¼ cup yellow cornmeal
- 2¼ cups bread flour
- 1½ teaspoons (1 packet) RED STAR® Active Dry Yeast or 1 teaspoon QUICK•RISE™ Yeast or Bread Machine Yeast

1½-POUND LOAF

- ½ cup water
- ¾ cup evaporated milk
- 3 tablespoons vegetable oil
- ⅛ teaspoon dried sweet marjoram
- ⅛ teaspoon ground ginger
- 1 teaspoon celery seed
- 1 teaspoon dried sage
- 1½ teaspoons salt
- 3 tablespoons sugar
- ⅓ cup yellow cornmeal
- 3 cups bread flour
- 2¼ teaspoons (1 packet) RED STAR® Active Dry Yeast or QUICK•RISE™ Yeast or Bread Machine Yeast

BREAD MACHINE METHOD

Have liquid ingredients at 80°F and all others at room temperature. Place ingredients in pan in order listed. Select basic cycle and medium/normal crust. Do not use delay timer. Check dough consistency after 5 minutes of kneading making adjustments if necessary.

MIXER METHODS

Using ingredient amounts listed for medium loaf, combine yeast, 1 cup flour and remaining dry ingredients. Combine liquids and heat to 120° to 130°F.

HAND-HELD MIXER METHOD

Combine dry mixture and liquid ingredients in mixing bowl on low speed. Beat 2 to 3 minutes on medium speed. Stir in enough remaining flour by hand to make firm dough. Knead on floured surface 5 to 7 minutes until smooth and elastic. Use additional flour if necessary.

STAND MIXER METHOD

Combine dry mixture and liquid ingredients in mixing bowl with paddle or beaters for 4 minutes on medium speed. Gradually add remaining flour and knead with dough hooks 5 to 7 minutes until smooth and elastic.

RISING, SHAPING AND BAKING

Place dough in lightly oiled bowl and turn to grease top. Cover; let rise until dough tests ripe.* Turn dough onto lightly floured surface; punch down to remove air bubbles. Roll or pat into a 14×7-inch rectangle. Starting with shorter side, roll up tightly, pressing dough into roll. Pinch edges and ends to seal. Place in greased 9×5-inch loaf pan. Cover; let rise until indentation remains after lightly touching dough. Bake in preheated 375°F oven 30 to 40 minutes. Remove from pan; cool on rack.   *Makes 1 loaf*

Place two fingers into the risen dough up to the second knuckle and take out. If the indentations remain, the dough is ripe and ready to punch down.

State Fair Cracked Wheat Bread

1⅓ cups water

2 tablespoons butter or margarine

1 teaspoon salt

¼ cup cracked wheat

3 cups bread flour

½ cup whole wheat flour

3 tablespoons nonfat dry milk powder

2 tablespoons firmly packed brown sugar

2 teaspoons FLEISCHMANN'S® Bread Machine Yeast

Add ingredients to bread machine pan in the order suggested by manufacturer. (If dough is too dry or stiff or too soft or slack, adjust dough consistency.) Recommended cycle: basic/white bread cycle; medium/normal crust color setting. *Makes 1 (2-pound) loaf*

tip:

It is extremely important to measure ingredients accurately when using a bread machine. As little as 1 tablespoon of liquid can make the difference between success and failure. Be sure to measure liquids at eye level and with the measuring cup on a flat surface.

State Fair Cracked Wheat Bread

Focaccia

1 cup water

1 tablespoon olive oil, plus additional for brushing

1 teaspoon salt

1 tablespoon sugar

3 cups bread flour

2¼ teaspoons (1 packet) RED STAR® Active Dry Yeast or QUICK•RISE™ Yeast or
Bread Machine Yeast

Suggested toppings: sun-dried tomatoes, roasted bell pepper slices, sautéed
onion rings, fresh and dried herbs in any combination, grated hard cheese

BREAD MACHINE METHOD

Place room temperature ingredients, except toppings, in pan in order listed. Select dough
cycle. Check dough consistency after 5 minutes of kneading, making adjustments if
necessary.

HAND-HELD MIXER METHOD

Combine yeast, 1 cup flour, sugar and salt. Combine water and 1 tablespoon oil; heat mixture
to 120° to 130°F. Combine dry and liquid mixtures in mixing bowl on low speed. Beat 2 to
3 minutes on medium speed. By hand, stir in enough remaining flour to make a firm dough.
Knead on floured surface 5 to 7 minutes or until smooth and elastic. Add additional flour,
if necessary.

STAND MIXER METHOD

Combine yeast, 1 cup flour, sugar and salt. Combine water and 1 tablespoon oil; heat
mixture to 120° to 130°F. Combine dry and liquid mixtures in mixing bowl with paddle or
beaters for 4 minutes on medium speed. Gradually add remaining flour and knead with
dough hook 5 to 7 minutes or until smooth and elastic. Add additional flour, if necessary.

continued on page 42

Focaccia

Focaccia, continued

FOOD PROCESSOR METHOD

In 2-cup measure, heat ¼ cup water to 110° to 115°F; keep remaining ¾ cup water cold. Add yeast; set aside. Insert dough blade in work bowl; add bread flour, sugar and salt. Pulse to combine. Add cold water and olive oil to yeast mixture; stir to combine. With machine running, add liquid mixture through feed tube in a steady stream only as fast as flour will absorb it. Open lid to check dough consistency. If dough is stiff and somewhat dry, add 1 teaspoon water; if soft and sticky, add 1 tablespoon flour. Close lid and process for 10 seconds. Check dough consistency again, making additional adjustments if necessary.

RISING, SHAPING AND BAKING

Place dough in lightly oiled bowl and turn to grease top. Cover; let rise until dough tests ripe.* Turn dough onto lightly floured surface; punch down to remove air bubbles. On lightly floured surface, shape dough into a ball. Place on greased baking sheet. Flatten to 14-inch circle. With knife, cut circle in dough about 1 inch from edge, cutting almost through to baking sheet. Pierce center with fork. Cover; let rise about 15 minutes. Brush with oil and sprinkle with desired toppings. Bake in preheated 375°F oven 25 to 30 minutes or until golden brown. Remove from baking sheet to cool. Serve warm or at room temperature.

Makes 1 (14-inch) loaf

*Place two fingers into the risen dough up to the second knuckle and take out. If the indentations remain, the dough is ripe and ready to punch down.

tip:

When flattening dough into circle, if it does not stretch easily, let dough rest a couple of minutes and then press it out. Repeat if necessary.

Golden Cheddar Batter Bread

1 package active dry yeast

¾ cup warm water (110° to 115°F)

3 cups unsifted all-purpose flour, divided

1½ cups finely chopped Golden Delicious apples

1 cup shredded Cheddar cheese

2 eggs, lightly beaten

2 tablespoons sugar

2 tablespoons vegetable shortening

1 teaspoon salt

Buttery Apple Spread (recipe follows)

1. In large bowl, combine yeast and water, stirring to dissolve yeast. Set aside until mixture begins to foam, about 5 minutes. Add 1½ cups flour, apples, cheese, eggs, sugar, shortening and salt to yeast mixture; beat with electric mixer at medium speed 2 minutes. Stir in remaining flour gradually with spoon. Cover with clean cloth and let rise 50 to 60 minutes or until doubled. Meanwhile, prepare Buttery Apple Spread.

2. Grease 9×5-inch loaf pan. Beat batter by hand 30 seconds. Spread batter evenly in prepared pan. Cover with cloth and let rise 40 minutes or until nearly doubled.

3. Heat oven to 375°F. Bake bread 45 to 55 minutes or until loaf sounds hollow when gently tapped. Remove from pan; cool on wire rack at least 15 minutes. Serve with Buttery Apple Spread. *Makes 1 loaf*

Buttery Apple Spread: Peel, core and slice 1 Golden Delicious apple; place in small saucepan with 1 tablespoon water. Cover tightly and cook over medium heat until apple is very tender. Mash apple with fork; cool completely. In small bowl, beat ½ cup softened butter with electric mixer until light and fluffy. Gradually add mashed apple; beat until well blended. Makes about 1 cup.

Favorite recipe from **Washington Apple Commission**

Challah

1-POUND LOAF

½ cup water

1 egg

2 tablespoons margarine, cut up

1 teaspoon salt

2 cups bread flour

1 tablespoon plus 1 teaspoon sugar

1½ teaspoons FLEISCHMANN'S® Bread Machine Yeast

1 egg yolk

1 tablespoon water

1½-POUND LOAF

¾ cup water

1 egg

3 tablespoons margarine, cut up

1¼ teaspoons salt

3 cups bread flour

2 tablespoons sugar

2 teaspoons FLEISCHMANN'S® Bread Machine Yeast

1 egg yolk

1 tablespoon water

Add water, egg, margarine, salt, bread flour, sugar and yeast to bread machine pan in the order suggested by manufacturer. Select dough/manual cycle. When cycle is complete, remove dough from machine to lightly floured surface. If necessary, knead in enough additional flour to make dough easy to handle. (For 1½-pound recipe, divide dough in half to make 2 loaves.)

For each loaf, divide dough into 2 pieces, one about ⅔ of the dough and the other about ⅓ of the dough. Divide larger piece into 3 equal pieces; roll into 12-inch ropes. Place ropes on

continued on page 46

Challah

Challah, continued

greased baking sheet. Braid by bringing left rope under center rope; lay it down. Bring right rope under new center rope; lay it down. Repeat to end. Pinch ends to seal. Divide remaining piece into 3 equal pieces. Roll into 10-inch ropes; braid. Place small braid on top of large braid. Pinch ends firmly to seal and secure large braid. Cover and let rise in warm, draft-free place until almost doubled in size, 15 to 20 minutes. Lightly beat egg yolk and 1 tablespoon water; brush over braids.

Bake at 375°F for 25 to 30 minutes or until done, covering with foil after 15 minutes to prevent excess browning. (For even browning when baking two loaves, switch positions of baking sheets halfway through baking.) Remove from baking sheets; cool on wire racks.

Makes 1 or 2 loaves

White Bread

2 packages active dry yeast

2¼ cups warm water (105° to 115°F), divided

6 to 6½ cups bread flour

⅓ cup instant dry milk

3 tablespoons sugar

2 tablespoons oil

1 tablespoon salt

Butter or margarine, softened

Dissolve yeast in ½ cup water in large bowl. Stir in remaining 1¾ cups water, 3 cups flour, dry milk, sugar, oil and salt; beat until smooth. Mix in enough remaining flour to make soft dough. Turn dough onto lightly floured surface; knead until smooth and elastic, about 12 to 15 minutes. Place dough in greased bowl, turning once to coat. Cover and let rise in warm place until doubled in size, about 1 hour.

Punch down dough; divide into halves. Roll each half into 18×9-inch rectangle. Fold crosswise into thirds, overlapping the two sides. Roll dough tightly toward you, jelly-roll style, beginning at one of the open ends. Press with thumbs to seal after each turn. Pinch edge firmly to seal. Press each end with side of hand to seal. Fold ends under loaves.

Place loaves seam sides down in two 9×5×3-inch greased loaf pans. Brush lightly with butter. Let rise until doubled in size, 50 to 60 minutes.

Preheat oven to 450°F. Place loaves on low rack so that tops of pans are in center of oven. (Pans should not touch each other or sides of oven.) Bake 10 minutes; reduce heat to 350°F and bake 30 to 35 minutes until deep golden brown and loaves sound hollow when tapped. Remove from pans. Brush loaves with butter; cool on wire rack.   *Makes 2 loaves*

Favorite recipe from **North Dakota Wheat Commission**

Garlic Herbed Pita Toasts

Preparation Time: 10 minutes
Total Time: 15 to 20 minutes

   4 (6-inch) pita breads (plain, whole wheat or flavored)
   ¼ cup CRISCO® Oil*
   1 teaspoon Italian seasoning
   ½ teaspoon salt
   ¼ teaspoon freshly ground black pepper
   ½ cup freshly grated Parmesan cheese

*Use your favorite Crisco Oil.

1. Heat oven to 425°F. Cover baking sheets with heavy duty aluminum foil.

2. Cut pita breads in half. Separate two layers of each half; you should have 16 pieces.

3. Brush each piece with oil. Sprinkle with Italian seasoning, salt, pepper and cheese. Arrange slices on baking sheets.

4. Bake at 425°F 5 to 7 minutes, or until brown and crisp. Serve warm.

Makes 4 to 6 servings

Note: Any combination of herbs can be used for this recipe. Any leftover toasts can be stored in air-tight containers for up to 3 days.

Potato Rosemary Rolls

DOUGH

1 cup plus 2 tablespoons water (70° to 80°F)

2 tablespoons olive oil

1 teaspoon salt

3 cups bread flour

½ cup instant potato flakes or buds

2 tablespoons nonfat dry milk powder

1 tablespoon sugar

1 teaspoon SPICE ISLANDS® Rosemary, crushed

1½ teaspoons FLEISCHMANN'S® Bread Machine Yeast

TOPPING

1 egg, lightly beaten

Sesame or poppy seeds or additional dried rosemary, crushed

Measure all dough ingredients into bread machine pan in the order suggested by manufacturer, adding potato flakes with flour. Select dough/manual cycle. When cycle is complete, remove dough to floured surface. If necessary, knead in additional flour to make dough easy to handle.

Divide dough into 12 equal pieces. Roll each piece to 10-inch rope; coil each rope and tuck end under coil. Place rolls 2 inches apart on large greased baking sheet. Cover; let rise in warm, draft-free place until doubled in size, about 45 to 60 minutes. Brush tops with beaten egg; sprinkle with sesame seeds. Bake at 375°F for 15 to 20 minutes or until done. Remove from pan; cool on wire rack. *Makes 12 rolls*

Note: Dough can be prepared in 1½- and 2-pound bread machines.

Potato Rosemary Rolls

Spicy Cheese Bread

   2 packages active dry yeast
   1 teaspoon granulated sugar
   ½ cup warm water (110°F)
 8¾ cups flour, divided
   3 cups shredded Jarlsberg or Swiss cheese
   2 tablespoons fresh chopped rosemary *or* 2 teaspoons dried rosemary
   1 tablespoon salt
   1 tablespoon TABASCO® brand Pepper Sauce
   2 cups milk
   4 eggs, lightly beaten

Combine yeast, sugar and warm water. Let stand 5 minutes until foamy. Meanwhile, combine 8 cups flour, cheese, rosemary, salt and TABASCO® Sauce in large bowl. Heat milk in small saucepan until warm (120° to 130°F).

Stir milk into flour mixture. Set aside 1 tablespoon beaten egg. Add remaining eggs to flour mixture with foamy yeast mixture; stir until soft dough forms.

Turn dough out onto lightly floured surface. Knead about 5 minutes, adding enough remaining flour to make a smooth and elastic dough. Shape dough into a ball; place in large greased bowl. Cover with towel and let rise in warm place until doubled, about 1½ hours.

Grease 2 large cookie sheets. Punch down dough and divide in half. Cut each half in 3 strips and braid. Place braided loaves on greased cookie sheets. Cover and let rise in warm place until almost doubled, 30 minutes to 1 hour. Preheat oven to 375°F. Brush loaves with reserved egg. Bake about 45 minutes or until loaves sound hollow when tapped. Remove to wire racks to cool. *Makes 2 loaves*

Spicy Cheese Bread

Shortcut "Sourdough" Corn Bread

1-POUND LOAF

  ½ cup plain low-fat yogurt

  ¼ cup milk

  1 tablespoon butter or margarine

  ¾ teaspoon salt

1¾ cups bread flour

  ⅓ cup cornmeal

  2 teaspoons sugar

1½ teaspoons FLEISCHMANN'S® Bread Machine Yeast

1½-POUND LOAF

  ⅔ cup plain low-fat yogurt

  ⅓ cup milk

  1 tablespoon butter or margarine

  1 teaspoon salt

2¾ cups bread flour

  ½ cup cornmeal

  1 tablespoon sugar

  2 teaspoons FLEISCHMANN'S® Bread Machine Yeast

Add ingredients to bread machine pan in the order suggested by manufacturer, adding yogurt with milk. (Yogurts vary in moisture content. If dough is too dry or stiff, or too soft or slack, adjust dough consistency—see Adjusting Dough Consistency tip below.) Recommended cycle: basic/white bread cycle; medium/normal crust color setting.

Makes 1 loaf (8 or 12 slices)

Adjusting Dough Consistency: Check dough after 5 minutes of mixing; it should form a soft, smooth ball around the blade. If dough is too stiff or dry, add additional liquid, 1 teaspoon at a time, until dough is of the right consistency. If dough is too soft or sticky, add additional bread flour, 1 teaspoon at a time.

Wisconsin Cheese Pull-Apart Bread

3 packages (about 3 dozen) frozen bread dough dinner rolls, thawed to room temperature

⅓ cup butter, melted

1 cup freshly grated Wisconsin Parmesan cheese

1 cup shredded Wisconsin Provolone cheese

Roll each dinner roll in butter, then in Parmesan cheese to coat. Arrange half the rolls in well-greased 12-cup fluted tube pan. Sprinkle with Provolone cheese. Top with remaining rolls. Sprinkle with any remaining Parmesan cheese. Let rise about 1 hour or until doubled in bulk.

Preheat oven to 375°F. Bake 35 to 45 minutes or until golden brown. Use table knife to loosen edges of bread. Remove from pan. Serve warm.   *Makes 12 servings*

Favorite recipe from **Wisconsin Milk Marketing Board**

tip:

Cover edges of bread with foil during last 10 to 15 minutes of baking if crust becomes too dark.

English Bath Buns

½ cup warm water (100° to 110°F)

2 envelopes FLEISCHMANN'S® Active Dry Yeast

½ cup warm milk (100° to 110°F)

½ cup (1 stick) butter or margarine, softened

2 tablespoons sugar

1 teaspoon salt

4 cups all-purpose flour

2 eggs

1 egg, lightly beaten with 1 tablespoon water

¼ cup sugar

1 cup chopped almonds

Place warm water in large warm bowl. Sprinkle in yeast; stir until dissolved. Add warm milk, butter, 2 tablespoons sugar, salt and 2 cups flour. Beat 2 minutes at medium speed of electric mixer. Add 2 eggs and ½ cup flour. Beat 2 minutes at high speed, scraping bowl occasionally. Stir in enough remaining flour to make soft dough. Knead on lightly floured surface until smooth and elastic, about 10 minutes. Place in greased bowl, turning to grease top. Cover; let rise in warm, draft-free place until doubled in size, about 1 hour.

Punch dough down; turn out onto lightly floured surface. Divide into 24 equal pieces. Shape each piece into smooth ball. Place in greased 2½-inch muffin cups. Cover; let rise in warm, draft-free place until doubled in size, about 30 minutes. Brush top with egg mixture. Sprinkle ¼ cup sugar and almonds over top. Bake at 375°F for 20 minutes or until done. Remove from pans; cool on wire racks.

Makes 24 buns

English Bath Buns

Freezer Rolls

1¼ cups warm water (100° to 110°F)
2 envelopes FLEISCHMANN'S® Active Dry Yeast
½ cup sugar
½ cup warm milk (100° to 110°F)
⅓ cup butter or margarine, softened
1½ teaspoons salt
5½ to 6 cups all-purpose flour
2 eggs

Place ½ cup warm water in large bowl. Sprinkle yeast over water; stir until dissolved. Add remaining ¾ cup warm water, sugar, warm milk, butter, salt and 2 cups flour. Beat 2 minutes at medium speed of electric mixer. Add eggs and ½ cup flour. Beat at high speed for 2 minutes. Stir in enough remaining flour to make soft dough. Turn out onto lightly floured surface. Knead until smooth and elastic, about 8 to 10 minutes. Cover with plastic wrap; let rest for 20 minutes.

Punch dough down. Shape into desired shapes for dinner rolls. Place on greased baking sheets. Cover with plastic wrap and foil, sealing well. Freeze up to 1 week.*

Once frozen, rolls may be placed in plastic freezer bags.

Remove rolls from freezer; unwrap and place on greased baking sheets. Cover; let rise in warm, draft-free place until doubled in size, about 1½ hours.

Bake at 350°F for 15 minutes or until done. Remove from baking sheets; cool on wire racks.

Makes about 2 dozen rolls

To bake without freezing: After shaping, let rise in warm, draft-free place until doubled in size, about 1 hour. Bake according to above directions.

Shaping the Dough: Crescents: Divide dough in half; roll each half to 14-inch circle. Cut each into 12 pie-shaped wedges. Roll up tightly from wide end. Curve ends slightly to form crescents. **Knots:** Divide dough into 24 equal pieces; roll each to 9-inch rope. Tie once loosely. **Coils:** Divide dough into 24 equal pieces; roll each to 9-inch rope. Coil each rope and tuck end under the coil. **Twists:** Divide dough into 24 equal pieces; roll each into 12-inch rope. Fold each rope in half and twist three to four times. Pinch ends to seal.

Freezer Rolls

Braided Sandwich Ring

DOUGH

¾ cup buttermilk, at 80°F

2 eggs, at room temperature

2 tablespoons vegetable oil

3 tablespoons sugar

1½ teaspoons salt

4 cups bread flour

2¼ teaspoons (1 packet) RED STAR® Active Dry Yeast or QUICK•RISE™ Yeast or Bread Machine Yeast

GLAZE

1 egg

1 tablespoon milk

1 tablespoon sesame or poppy seeds

FILLING

Mayonnaise, leaf lettuce, sliced tomatoes, onion rings, sliced black olives, thinly sliced deli meats (ham, roast beef, prosciutto, salami), sliced cheeses (brick, mozzarella, Swiss), Dijon mustard

BREAD MACHINE METHOD

Place room temperature dough ingredients in pan in order listed. Select dough cycle. Check dough consistency after 5 minutes of kneading making adjustments if necessary.

HAND-HELD MIXER METHOD

Combine 2 cups flour, sugar, yeast and salt. Heat buttermilk to 120° to 130°F. Combine flour mixture, buttermilk, 2 eggs and oil in mixing bowl on low speed. Beat 2 to 3 minutes on medium speed. By hand, stir in enough remaining flour to make firm dough. Knead on floured surface 5 to 7 minutes or until smooth and elastic. Use additional flour, if necessary. Place dough in lightly oiled bowl and turn to grease top. Cover; let rise until dough tests ripe.*

STAND MIXER METHOD

Combine 2 cups flour, sugar, yeast and salt. Heat buttermilk to 120° to 130°F. Combine flour mixture, buttermilk, 2 eggs and oil in mixing bowl with paddle or beaters 4 minutes on medium speed. Gradually add remaining flour and knead with dough hook 5 to 7 minutes or until smooth and elastic. Use additional flour, if necessary. Place dough in lightly oiled bowl and turn to grease top. Cover; let rise until dough tests ripe.*

SHAPING AND BAKING

Punch down dough. Divide into three parts. On lightly floured surface, roll each third into 24-inch rope. On greased baking sheet lightly sprinkled with cornmeal, loosely braid ropes from center to ends. Shape into circle; fasten ends by pinching dough together. Cover; let rise until indentation remains after touching.

For glaze, combine remaining 1 egg and milk; gently brush risen dough. Sprinkle with sesame seeds. Bake in preheated 375°F oven 25 to 35 minutes or until golden brown; cool.

Using serrated knife, slice ring crosswise to create large sandwich. Spread bottom half with mayonnaise; arrange filling ingredients. Spread top section with mustard; place on top of filling. To serve slice into serving portions.

Makes 1 large sandwich ring (12 to 18 servings)

Place two fingers into the risen dough up to the second knuckle and take out. If the indentations remain, the dough is ripe and ready to punch down.

tip:

For the best baking results, place the bread on the center rack of a preheated oven. The bread is done when it is golden brown, well-rounded, and sounds hollow when lightly tapped. For a crisp crust, place a pan of water in the bottom of the oven during baking, or brush the top of the bread with water. For a softer crust, brush with softened butter immediately after baking.

Bread Bowls

1¼ cups water

1 teaspoon salt

1½ teaspoons sugar

3 tablespoons white cornmeal

3¾ cups bread flour

2¼ teaspoons (1 packet) RED STAR® Active Dry Yeast or QUICK•RISE™ Yeast or
Bread Machine Yeast

BREAD MACHINE METHOD

Place room temperature ingredients in pan in order listed. Select dough cycle. Check
dough consistency after 5 minutes of kneading, making adjustments, if necessary.

TRADITIONAL METHOD

Combine yeast, 1 cup flour and other dry ingredients. Heat water to 120° to 130°F; add to flour
mixture. Beat 3 minutes on medium speed. By hand, stir in enough remaining flour to make
firm dough. Knead on floured surface 5 to 7 minutes until smooth and elastic. Use additional
flour, if necessary. Place dough in lightly greased bowl. Cover; let rise until dough tests ripe.*

SHAPING, RISING AND BAKING

Turn dough onto lightly floured surface; punch down to remove air bubbles. Divide and
shape into three round balls. Place on greased baking sheet covered with cornmeal. Cover;
let rise until indentation remains after lightly touching sides of bowls. Bake in preheated
425°F oven 20 to 30 minutes. Spray or brush loaf with cold water several times during first
10 minutes of baking for a crispy crust. Remove from baking sheet; cool.

TO MAKE BOWLS

Cut thin slice off the top. Hollow out inside, leaving half-inch sides. Placing bowls in a
300°F oven for 10 minutes will dry sides and prevent premature soaking from the salads
and soups.   *Makes 3 bread bowls*

*Place two fingers into the risen dough up to the second knuckle and take out. If the indentations
remain, the dough is ripe and ready to punch down.*

Bread Bowls

Holiday Rye Bread

   3 to 3½ cups all-purpose flour
2½ cups rye flour
   ⅓ cup sugar
   2 envelopes FLEISCHMANN'S® RapidRise™ Yeast
2½ teaspoons salt
   1 tablespoon grated orange peel
   2 teaspoons fennel seed
   1 cup beer or malt liquor
   ½ cup water
   ¼ cup light molasses
   2 tablespoons butter or margarine
   Molasses Glaze (recipe follows)

In large bowl, combine 1½ cups all-purpose flour, rye flour, sugar, undissolved yeast, salt, orange peel and fennel seed. Heat beer, water, molasses and butter until very warm (120° to 130°F). Stir into dry ingredients. Beat 2 minutes at medium speed of electric mixer, scraping bowl occasionally. Stir in enough remaining flour to make soft dough. Knead on lightly floured surface until smooth and elastic, about 8 to 10 minutes. Cover; let rest 10 minutes.

Divide dough into 4 equal pieces. Roll each to 10×6-inch oval. Roll each up tightly from long side, as for jelly roll, tapering ends. Pinch seams to seal. Place on greased baking sheets. Cover; let rise in warm, draft-free place until doubled in size, about 1½ hours.

With sharp knife, make 3 diagonal cuts on top of each loaf. Brush with Molasses Glaze. Bake at 375°F for 15 minutes; brush loaves with Glaze. Bake additional 10 minutes or until done. Remove loaves from oven and brush again with Glaze. Cool on wire racks.

Makes 4 small loaves

Molasses Glaze: Combine 2 tablespoons molasses and 2 tablespoons water. Stir until well blended.

Savory Cheese Bread

  6 to 7 cups flour, divided
  2 tablespoons sugar
  4 teaspoons instant minced onion
  2 teaspoons salt
  2 packages active dry yeast
  ½ teaspoon caraway seeds
 1¾ cups milk
  ½ cup water
  3 tablespoons butter or margarine
  1 teaspoon TABASCO® brand Pepper Sauce
  2 cups (8 ounces) shredded sharp Cheddar cheese, divided
  1 egg, lightly beaten

Combine 2½ cups flour, sugar, onion, salt, yeast and caraway seeds in large bowl of electric mixer. Combine milk, water and butter in small saucepan. Heat milk mixture until very warm (120° to 130°F); stir in TABASCO® Sauce.

With mixer at medium speed, gradually add milk mixture to dry ingredients; beat 2 minutes. Add 1 cup flour. Beat at high speed 2 minutes. With wooden spoon stir in 1½ cups cheese and enough flour to make a stiff dough. Turn dough out onto lightly floured surface. Knead 8 to 10 minutes or until dough is smooth and elastic, adding as much remaining flour as needed to prevent sticking. Place dough in large greased bowl and turn once to grease surface. Cover with towel; let rise in warm place (90° to 100°F) 1 hour or until doubled in bulk.

Punch dough down. Divide dough into 16 equal pieces; shape each piece into a ball. Place half the balls in well-greased 10-inch tube pan. Sprinkle with remaining ½ cup cheese. Arrange remaining balls on top. Cover with towel; let rise in warm place 45 minutes or until doubled in bulk. Preheat oven to 375°F. Brush dough with egg. Bake 40 to 50 minutes or until golden brown. Remove from pan. Cool completely on wire rack.

Makes 1 (10-inch) round loaf

Honey of a Whole Wheat Bread

1-POUND LOAF

¼ cup water

¼ cup milk

1 egg, at room temperature

2 tablespoons honey

2 teaspoons butter, cut into small pieces

1½ teaspoons salt

⅔ cup whole wheat flour

1⅓ cups bread flour

1½ teaspoons RED STAR® Active Dry Yeast or 1 teaspoon QUICK•RISE™ Yeast or Bread Machine Yeast

1½-POUND LOAF

¼ cup water

½ cup milk

1 egg, at room temperature

¼ cup honey

1 tablespoon butter, cut into small pieces

2 teaspoons salt

1 cup whole wheat flour

2 cups bread flour

2¼ teaspoons (1 packet) RED STAR® Active Dry Yeast or 1½ teaspoons QUICK•RISE™ Yeast or Bread Machine Yeast

BREAD MACHINE DIRECTIONS

Place room temperature ingredients in pan in order listed. Select basic/white cycle, medium crust. Do not use delay timer. Check dough consistency after 5 minutes of kneading making adjustments, if necessary. Cool on rack.   *Makes 1 loaf*

Honey of a Whole Wheat Bread

Good Old American White Rolls

¾ cup milk

¼ cup (½ stick) butter

2 eggs

1 teaspoon salt

¼ cup sugar

3 cups bread flour

2¼ teaspoons (1 packet) RED STAR® Active Dry Yeast or QUICK•RISE™ Yeast or Bread Machine Yeast

BREAD MACHINE METHOD

Place room temperature ingredients in pan in order listed. Select dough cycle. Do not use the delay timer. Check dough consistency after 5 minutes of kneading, making adjustments, if necessary.

HAND-HELD MIXER METHOD

Combine yeast, 1 cup flour, sugar and salt. Heat milk and butter to 120° to 130°F (butter does not need to melt). Combine dry mixture, milk and butter in mixing bowl on low speed. Beat 2 to 3 minutes on medium speed. Add room temperature eggs; beat 1 minute. By hand, stir in enough remaining flour to make a firm dough. Knead on floured surface 5 to 7 minutes or until smooth and elastic. Add additional flour, if necessary.

STAND MIXER METHOD

Combine yeast, 1 cup flour, sugar and salt. Heat milk and butter to 120° to 130°F (butter does not need to melt). Combine dry mixture, milk and butter in mixer bowl with paddle or beaters for 4 minutes on medium speed. Add room temperature eggs; beat 1 minute. Gradually add flour and knead with dough hooks 5 to 7 minutes or until smooth and elastic. Add additional flour, if necessary.

FOOD PROCESSOR METHOD

Divide milk. In a 2-cup measure, heat ¼ cup milk to 110° to 115°F; add yeast and set aside. Insert dough blade in work bowl; add bread flour, sugar and salt. Pulse to combine. Have butter, eggs and remaining ½ cup milk cold. Add cold butter, eggs and milk to yeast mixture; stir to combine. With machine running, add liquid mixture through feed tube in a steady stream only as fast as flour will absorb it. Open lid to check dough consistency. If dough is stiff and somewhat dry, add 1 teaspoon water; if soft and sticky, add 1 tablespoon flour. Check dough consistency again, making additional adjustments if necessary. Once dough forms a ball, continue processing for 10 seconds to knead dough.

RISING, SHAPING AND BAKING
Place dough in lightly oiled bowl and turn to grease top. Cover; let rise until dough tests ripe.* Divide dough into 4 parts; divide each part into 3 pieces. For pan rolls, shape each piece into smooth ball, place in greased 9-inch cake pan. For individual rolls, place balls in greased muffin pan cups or 2 to 3 inches apart on greased baking sheet. Cover; let rise at room temperature until indentation remains when touched. Bake in preheated 375°F oven: pan rolls, 20 to 25 minutes; individual rolls, 12 to 15 minutes. If desired, lightly brush with butter. Remove from pan and cool. *Makes 1 dozen rolls*

Place two fingers into the risen dough up to the second knuckle and take out. If the indentations remain, the dough is ripe and ready to punch down.

Savory French Bread

1 large loaf French bread
¼ cup (½ stick) butter or margarine, softened
½ teaspoon dried basil leaves
½ teaspoon dried dill weed
½ teaspoon chopped dried chives
¼ teaspoon garlic powder
¼ teaspoon paprika
½ teaspoon TABASCO® brand Pepper Sauce

Preheat oven to 400°F. Slice bread diagonally, but do not cut through bottom crust of loaf. Mix remaining ingredients in small bowl. Spread between bread slices; wrap bread in aluminum foil and heat in oven for 15 to 20 minutes. Serve warm. *Makes 6 to 8 servings*

1-2-3 Steak Soup *(page 95)*

Golden Tomato Soup *(page 94)*

soups & stews

Enjoy steaming bowls of hearty soups and stews that will fill you up and keep you warm.

Taco Soup *(page 83)*

Chicken Tortilla Soup

Prep Time: 5 minutes
Cook Time: 6 minutes

1 clove garlic, minced
1 can (14½ ounces) chicken broth
1 jar (16 ounces) mild chunky-style salsa
2 tablespoons *Frank's® RedHot®* Original Cayenne Pepper Sauce
1 package (10 ounces) fully cooked carved chicken breasts
1 can (8¾ ounces) whole kernel corn, undrained
1 tablespoon chopped fresh cilantro (optional)
1 cup crushed tortilla chips
½ cup (2 ounces) shredded Monterey Jack cheese

1. Heat *1 teaspoon oil* in large saucepan over medium-high heat. Cook garlic 1 minute or until tender. Add broth, *¾ cup water,* salsa and **Frank's RedHot** Sauce. Stir in chicken, corn and cilantro. Heat to boiling. Reduce heat to medium-low. Cook, covered, 5 minutes.

2. Stir in tortilla chips and cheese. Serve hot. *Makes 4 servings*

Chicken Tortilla Soup

Sausage & Zucchini Soup

1 pound BOB EVANS® Italian Roll Sausage

1 medium onion, diced

1 (28-ounce) can stewed tomatoes

2 (14-ounce) cans beef broth

2 medium zucchini, sliced or diced (about 2 cups)

2 small carrots, diced

2 stalks celery, diced

4 large mushrooms, sliced

Grated Parmesan cheese for garnish

Crumble and cook sausage and onion in large saucepan over medium heat until sausage is browned. Drain off any drippings. Add remaining ingredients except cheese; simmer, uncovered, over low heat about 40 minutes or until vegetables are tender. Garnish with cheese. Refrigerate leftovers. *Makes 8 servings*

Country Vegetable Soup

3 cans (13¾ ounces each) chicken broth

1 cup water

1 package (4½ ounces) creamy chicken, rice and sauce mix

½ teaspoon dried basil

1 bag (16 ounces) BIRDS EYE® frozen Farm Fresh Mixtures Broccoli, Green Beans, Pearl Onions and Red Peppers

• Bring broth, water, rice and sauce mix and basil to a boil in large saucepan over high heat.

• Reduce heat to medium. Cook, uncovered, 7 minutes.

• Add vegetables; cook 6 to 7 minutes or until rice and vegetables are tender.

Makes 4 servings

Sausage & Zucchini Soup

Tortellini Soup

3 cloves garlic, minced

1 tablespoon butter or margarine

1 can (48 ounces) COLLEGE INN® Chicken or Beef Broth

1 package (about 19 ounces) frozen cheese tortellini

1 package (10 ounces) frozen chopped spinach, thawed

2 cans (14½ ounces each) stewed tomatoes, undrained, cut into pieces
   Grated Parmesan cheese

In large saucepan over medium-high heat, cook garlic in butter for 1 to 2 minutes. Add broth and tortellini. Heat to a boil; reduce heat and simmer 10 minutes. Add spinach and tomatoes; simmer 5 minutes longer. Sprinkle each serving with cheese.

Makes 8 to 10 servings (about 11 cups)

Zesty Black-Eyed Pea Soup

4 strips bacon, chopped

1 cup chopped onion

2 cloves garlic, minced

2 cans (15½ ounces *each*) black-eyed peas, undrained

1 can (14½ ounces) chicken broth

3 tablespoons *Frank's® RedHot®* Original Cayenne Pepper Sauce

1 teaspoon dried thyme leaves

1. Cook and stir bacon in large saucepan over medium-high heat 5 minutes or until crisp. Transfer to dish. Add onion and garlic to saucepan; cook and stir 3 minutes or until tender.

2. Stir in remaining ingredients. Add *½ cup water*. Heat to boiling. Reduce heat to medium-low. Cook 15 minutes, stirring occasionally. Sprinkle reserved bacon on top of soup before serving.

Makes 6 (1-cup) servings

Tortellini Soup

Mushroom and Rice Soup

1 bag SUCCESS® Rice

2 tablespoons olive oil

2 cups sliced fresh mushrooms

1 cup chopped onion

1 cup diagonally sliced green onions

5 cups chicken broth

1 teaspoon black pepper

1 teaspoon dried thyme leaves, crushed

1 tablespoon dry sherry

Prepare rice according to package directions.

Heat oil in large saucepan or Dutch oven over medium heat. Add mushrooms and onion; cook and stir until tender. Add broth, pepper and thyme. Reduce heat to low; simmer until thoroughly heated, 5 to 7 minutes. Stir in rice and sherry; heat thoroughly, stirring occasionally. Garnish, if desired.

Makes 4 servings

Mushroom and Rice Soup

Black Bean & Pork Stew

2 (15-ounce) cans cooked black beans, rinsed and drained

2 cups water

1 pound boneless ham, cut into ¾-inch cubes

¾ pound BOB EVANS® Italian Dinner Link Sausage, cut into 1-inch pieces

¾ pound BOB EVANS® Smoked Sausage, cut into 1-inch pieces

1 pint cherry tomatoes, stems removed

1 medium onion, chopped

1 teaspoon red pepper flakes

6 cloves garlic, minced

⅛ teaspoon grated orange peel

Cornbread or rolls (optional)

Preheat oven to 350°F. Combine all ingredients except cornbread in large Dutch oven. Bring to a boil over high heat, skimming foam off if necessary. Cover; transfer to oven. Bake 30 minutes; uncover and bake 30 minutes more, stirring occasionally. Serve hot with cornbread, if desired, or cool slightly, then cover and refrigerate overnight. To serve, remove any fat from surface. Reheat over low heat and refrigerate any leftovers.

Makes 8 servings

Black Bean & Pork Stew

Ravioli Soup

Prep and Cook Time: 15 minutes

> 1 package (9 ounces) fresh or frozen cheese ravioli or tortellini
> ¾ pound hot Italian sausage, crumbled
> 1 can (14½ ounces) DEL MONTE® Stewed Tomatoes - Seasoned with Basil,
>   Garlic & Oregano
> 1 can (14½ ounces) beef broth
> 1 can (14½ ounces) DEL MONTE® Italian Beans, drained
> 2 green onions, sliced

1. Cook pasta according to package directions; drain.

2. Meanwhile, cook sausage in 5-quart pot over medium-high heat until no longer pink; drain. Add undrained tomatoes, broth and 1¾ cups water; bring to a boil.

3. Reduce heat to low; stir in pasta, beans and green onions. Simmer until heated through. Season with pepper and sprinkle with grated Parmesan cheese, if desired.

Makes 4 servings

Ravioli Soup

Tortilla Soup

1 tablespoon butter or margarine

½ cup chopped green bell pepper

½ cup chopped onion

½ teaspoon ground cumin

3½ cups (two 14½-ounce cans) chicken broth

1 jar (16 ounces) ORTEGA® Salsa-Thick & Chunky

1 cup whole-kernel corn

1 tablespoon vegetable oil

6 corn tortillas, cut into ½-inch strips

¾ cup (3 ounces) shredded 4-cheese Mexican blend

Sour cream (optional)

MELT butter in medium saucepan over medium heat. Add bell pepper, onion and cumin; cook for 3 to 4 minutes or until tender. Stir in broth, salsa and corn. Bring to a boil. Reduce heat to low; cook for 5 minutes.

HEAT vegetable oil in medium skillet over medium-high heat. Add tortilla strips; cook for 3 to 4 minutes or until crisp.

SERVE in soup bowls. Top with tortilla strips, cheese and a dollop of sour cream.

Makes 6 servings

Taco Soup

  1 pound BOB EVANS® Original Recipe or
     Zesty Hot Roll Sausage
1½ tablespoons olive oil
  ½ small Spanish onion, diced
  1 jalapeño pepper,* seeded and diced
1½ cups beef broth
  1 cup peeled, seeded and diced fresh or canned tomatoes
  1 cup vegetable juice
1½ teaspoons ground cumin
1½ teaspoons chili powder
  ¼ teaspoon salt
  ⅓ cup shredded Cheddar cheese
 12 tortilla chips, broken into pieces

Jalapeño peppers can sting and irritate the skin; wear rubber gloves when handling peppers and do not touch eyes. Wash hands after handling.

Crumble and cook sausage in olive oil in Dutch oven until no longer pink but not yet browned. Add onion and pepper; cook until onion is tender. Add remaining ingredients except cheese and chips; bring to a boil over high heat. Reduce heat to low and simmer, uncovered, 15 minutes. Ladle soup into bowls; garnish with cheese and chips. Refrigerate leftovers. *Makes 6 servings*

Hearty Sausage Stew

¼ cup olive oil

4 carrots, chopped

1 onion, cut into quarters

1 cup chopped celery

2 cloves garlic, finely chopped

1 teaspoon finely chopped fennel

Salt and black pepper to taste

12 small new potatoes

1 pound mushrooms, cut into halves

2 cans (12 ounces each) diced tomatoes, undrained

1 can (8 ounces) tomato sauce

1 tablespoon dried oregano leaves

1 pound HILLSHIRE FARM® Polska Kielbasa,* sliced

Or use any variety Hillshire Farm® Smoked Sausage.

Heat oil in heavy skillet over medium-high heat; add carrots, onion, celery, garlic, fennel, salt and pepper. Sauté until vegetables are soft. Add potatoes, mushrooms, tomatoes with liquid, tomato sauce and oregano; cook 20 minutes over low heat. Add Polska Kielbasa; simmer 15 minutes or until heated through.   *Makes 6 servings*

tip:

Did you know? If you don't have 2 cups of tomato sauce, you can substitute with ¾ cup of tomato paste mixed into 1 cup of water.

Hearty Sausage Stew

Classic Onion Soup

4 large yellow onions (about 9 to 11 ounces each), sliced

6 tablespoons butter or margarine

1 tablespoon sugar

2 quarts reduced-sodium chicken broth

½ cup brandy (optional)

Salt and black pepper to taste

½ baguette French bread, cut into slices and toasted

Grated Romano cheese

Melt butter in 4-quart saucepan or Dutch oven. Add onions; cook over medium heat 12 minutes, stirring often, or until tender and golden. Add sugar and cook, stirring for 1 minute. Add broth; cover and bring to a boil. Reduce heat; simmer 12 minutes. If desired, add brandy; cook 2 minutes longer. Season with salt and pepper. To serve, ladle soup into bowl; float toast on top. Sprinkle with cheese. *Makes 6 servings*

Favorite recipe from **National Onion Association**

Classic Onion Soup

Southwestern Beef Stew

1 tablespoon plus 1 teaspoon BERTOLLI® Olive Oil, divided
1½ pounds boneless beef chuck, cut into 1-inch cubes
1 can (4 ounces) chopped green chilies, drained
2 large cloves garlic, finely chopped
1 teaspoon ground cumin (optional)
1 can (14 to 16 ounces) whole or plum tomatoes, undrained and chopped
1 envelope LIPTON® RECIPE SECRETS® Onion or Beefy Onion Soup Mix
1 cup water
1 package (10 ounces) frozen cut okra or green beans, thawed
1 large red or green bell pepper, cut into 1-inch pieces
4 frozen half-ears corn-on-the-cob, thawed and each cut into 3 round pieces
2 tablespoons chopped fresh cilantro (optional)

In 5-quart Dutch oven or heavy saucepot, heat 1 tablespoon oil over medium-high heat and brown ½ of the beef; remove and set aside. Repeat with remaining beef; remove and set aside. In same Dutch oven, heat remaining 1 teaspoon oil over medium heat and cook chilies, garlic and cumin, stirring constantly, 3 minutes. Return beef to Dutch oven. Stir in tomatoes and onion soup mix blended with water. Bring to a boil over high heat. Reduce heat to low and simmer covered, stirring occasionally, for 1 hour. Stir in okra, red pepper and corn. Bring to a boil over high heat. Reduce heat to low and simmer covered, stirring occasionally, for 30 minutes or until meat is tender. Sprinkle with cilantro.

Makes 6 servings

Southwestern Beef Stew

Vegetable Soup

2 tablespoons FILIPPO BERIO® Olive Oil

2 medium potatoes, peeled and quartered

2 medium onions, sliced

3 cups beef broth

8 ounces fresh green beans, trimmed and cut into 1-inch pieces

3 carrots, peeled and chopped

8 ounces fresh spinach, washed, drained, stemmed and chopped

1 green bell pepper, diced

2 tablespoons chopped fresh parsley

1 tablespoon chopped fresh basil *or* 1 teaspoon dried basil

½ teaspoon ground cumin

1 clove garlic, finely minced

   Salt and freshly ground black pepper

In Dutch oven, heat olive oil over medium-high heat until hot. Add potatoes and onions; cook and stir 5 minutes. Add beef broth, green beans and carrots. Bring mixture to a boil. Cover; reduce heat to low and simmer 10 minutes, stirring occasionally. Add spinach, bell pepper, parsley, basil, cumin and garlic. Cover; simmer an additional 15 to 20 minutes or until potatoes are tender. Season to taste with salt and black pepper. Serve hot.

Makes 6 to 8 servings

Vegetable Soup

Oniony Mushroom Soup

Prep Time: 20 minutes
Cook Time: 18 minutes

    2 cans (10¾ ounces each) condensed golden mushroom soup
    1 can (13¾ ounces) reduced-sodium beef broth
  1⅓ cups *French's*® French Fried Onions, divided
    ½ cup water
    ⅓ cup dry sherry wine
    4 slices French bread, cut ½ inch thick
    1 tablespoon olive oil
    1 clove garlic, finely minced
    1 cup (4 ounces) shredded Swiss cheese

Combine mushroom soup, beef broth, *1 cup* French Fried Onions, water and sherry in large saucepan. Bring to a boil over medium-high heat, stirring often. Reduce heat to low. Simmer 15 minutes, stirring occasionally.

Preheat broiler. Place bread on baking sheet. Combine oil and garlic in small bowl. Brush oil over both sides of bread slices. Broil bread until toasted and crisp, turning once.

Ladle soup into 4 broiler-safe bowls. Place 1 slice of bread in each bowl. Sprinkle evenly with cheese and remaining *⅓ cup* onions. Place bowls on baking sheet. Place under broiler about 1 minute or until cheese is melted and onions are golden. *Makes 4 servings*

tip:

Make all your soups special by topping with *French's*® French Fried Onions. They'll give your soup a wonderful oniony flavor.

Oniony Mushroom Soup

Golden Tomato Soup

4 teaspoons margarine

1 cup chopped onion

2 cloves garlic, coarsely chopped

½ cup chopped carrot

¼ cup chopped celery

8 medium Florida tomatoes, blanched, peeled,
  seeded and chopped

6 cups chicken broth

¼ cup uncooked rice

2 tablespoons tomato paste

1 tablespoon Worcestershire sauce

½ teaspoon dried thyme leaves, crushed

¼ to ½ teaspoon ground black pepper

5 drops hot pepper sauce

Melt margarine in large Dutch oven over medium-high heat. Add onion and garlic; cook and stir 1 to 2 minutes or until onion is tender. Add carrots and celery; cook and stir 7 to 9 minutes or until tender, stirring frequently. Stir in tomatoes, broth, rice, tomato paste, Worcestershire sauce, thyme, black pepper and hot pepper sauce. Reduce heat to low; cook about 30 minutes, stirring frequently. Remove from heat. Let cool about 10 minutes.

In food processor or blender, process soup in small batches until smooth. Return soup to Dutch oven; simmer 3 to 5 minutes or until heated through. Garnish as desired.

Makes 8 servings

Favorite recipe from **Florida Tomato Committee**

1-2-3 Steak Soup

Prep Time: 5 minutes
Cook Time: 30 minutes

  1 pound boneless beef sirloin steak, cut into 1-inch cubes
  1 tablespoon vegetable oil
  ½ pound sliced mushrooms (about 2½ cups)
  2 cups *French's*® French Fried Onions, divided
  1 package (16 ounces) frozen vegetables for stew (potatoes, carrots, celery and
      pearl onions)
  2 cans (14½ ounces each) beef broth
  1 can (8 ounces) tomato sauce
  1 tablespoon *French's*® Worcestershire Sauce
    Garnish: chopped parsley (optional)

1. Cook beef in hot oil in large saucepan over medium heat until browned, stirring
frequently. Remove beef from pan; set aside.

2. Sauté mushrooms and ⅔ *cup* French Fried Onions in drippings in same pan over
medium heat until golden, stirring occasionally. Stir in vegetables, broth, tomato sauce and
Worcestershire. Return beef to pan.

3. Heat to a boil over high heat; reduce heat to low. Cover and simmer 20 minutes or until
vegetables are tender, stirring occasionally. Spoon soup into serving bowls; top with
remaining onions. Garnish with chopped parsley, if desired.   *Makes 8 servings*

Oven-Roasted Vegetables *(page 115)*

Creamy Spinach Italiano *(page 125)*

Grilled, baked, sautéed or scalloped—these vegetable dishes are guaranteed to please everyone at the dinner table.

on the side

Zippy Oven Fries *(page 120)*

Scalloped Garlic Potatoes

   3 medium all-purpose potatoes, peeled and thinly sliced (about 1½ pounds)
   1 envelope LIPTON® RECIPE SECRETS® Savory Herb with Garlic Soup Mix
   1 cup (½ pint) whipping or heavy cream
   ½ cup water

1. Preheat oven to 375°F. In lightly greased 2-quart shallow baking dish, arrange potatoes. In medium bowl, blend remaining ingredients; pour over potatoes.

2. Bake, uncovered, 45 minutes or until potatoes are tender.   *Makes 4 servings*

Honey-Glazed Sweet Potatoes

   1½ pounds sweet potatoes or yams, peeled and quartered
   ⅔ cup orange juice, divided
   ½ teaspoon ground ginger
   ½ teaspoon ground nutmeg
   1 tablespoon butter or margarine
   1 tablespoon cornstarch
   ⅓ cup honey

MICROWAVE DIRECTIONS

Combine sweet potatoes and ⅓ cup orange juice in 2-quart microwave-safe baking dish; sprinkle with ginger and nutmeg. Dot with butter. Cover and microwave at HIGH (100%) 7 to 10 minutes or until sweet potatoes are tender, stirring halfway through cooking time. Combine cornstarch, remaining ⅓ cup orange juice and honey in medium microwave-safe bowl. Microwave at HIGH 2 minutes or until thickened, stirring every 30 seconds. Drain liquid from sweet potatoes; add to honey mixture. Microwave at HIGH 1 minute. Pour sauce over sweet potatoes and microwave at HIGH 1 minute more or until sweet potatoes are thoroughly heated.   *Makes 4 servings*

Favorite recipe from **National Honey Board**

Scalloped Garlic Potatoes

1-2-3 Cheddar Broccoli Casserole

Prep Time: 5 minutes
Cook Time: 20 minutes

> 1 jar (1 pound) RAGÚ® Cheesy!® Double Cheddar Sauce
> 2 boxes (10 ounces each) frozen broccoli florets, thawed
> ¼ cup plain or Italian seasoned dry bread crumbs
> 1 tablespoon I CAN'T BELIEVE IT'S NOT BUTTER!® Spread, melted

Preheat oven to 350°F. In 1½-quart casserole, combine Ragú Cheesy! Sauce and broccoli.

Evenly top with bread crumbs combined with Spread.

Bake, uncovered, 20 minutes or until bread crumbs are golden and broccoli is tender.

Makes 6 servings

Variation: Substitute your favorite frozen vegetables or vegetable blend for broccoli florets.

Honey-Glazed Carrots

> 3 cups sliced carrots
> 6 tablespoons honey
> 2 tablespoons butter or margarine
> 2 tablespoons chopped fresh parsley
> 1½ teaspoons Dijon mustard (optional)

Bring 2 inches of salted water to a boil in medium saucepan over high heat. Add carrots and return to a boil. Reduce heat to medium. Cover and cook 8 to 12 minutes or until carrots are crisp-tender. Drain carrots; return to saucepan. Stir in honey, butter, parsley and mustard, if desired. Cook and stir over low heat until carrots are glazed.

Makes 6 servings

Favorite recipe from **National Honey Board**

1-2-3 Cheddar Broccoli Casserole

Double Cheddar Scalloped Potatoes

Prep Time: 10 minutes
Cook Time: 35 minutes

> 1 package (5 ounces) scalloped potato mix
> 2 cups boiling water
> 1 cup (4 ounces) shredded Cheddar cheese
> ¾ cup milk
> ¼ cup cooked crumbled bacon
> 1⅓ cups *French's*® French Fried Onions, divided
>   Garnish: chopped parsley (optional)

1. Preheat oven to 400°F. Stir potato mix, sauce mix and boiling water in ungreased 1-quart casserole. Add cheese, milk, bacon and ⅔ *cup* French Fried Onions; stir until well blended.

2. Bake, uncovered, 35 minutes or until top is golden and potatoes are tender.

3. Top with remaining onions. Let stand a few minutes for sauce to thicken. Garnish with parsley, if desired.

Makes 6 servings

tip:

Stir in ¼ cup chopped green onions for an extra flavor boost.

Original Green Bean Casserole

Prep Time: 5 minutes
Cook Time: 35 minutes

> 1 can (10¾ ounces) condensed cream of mushroom soup
> ¾ cup milk
> ⅛ teaspoon ground black pepper
> 2 packages (9 ounces each) frozen cut green beans, thawed and drained *or* 2 cans
>   (14½ ounces each) cut green beans, drained
> 1⅓ cups *French's*® French Fried Onions, divided

Preheat oven to 350°F. Combine soup, milk and ground pepper in 1½-quart casserole; stir until well blended. Stir in beans and ⅔ *cup* French Fried Onions.

Bake, uncovered, 30 minutes or until hot. Stir; sprinkle with remaining ⅔ *cup* onions. Bake 5 minutes or until onions are golden.   *Makes 6 servings*

Microwave Directions: Prepare green bean mixture as above; pour into 1½-quart microwave-safe casserole. Cook, covered, on HIGH 8 to 10 minutes or until heated through. Stir beans halfway through cooking time. Top with remaining French Fried Onions; cook, uncovered, 1 minute. Let stand 5 minutes.

Grilled Vegetable Platter

Prep Time: 10 minutes
Marinating Time: 30 minutes
Cook Time: 10 to 12 minutes

   1 cup LAWRY'S® Herb & Garlic Marinade With Lemon Juice
12 small portabello mushrooms, cut into ½-inch slices
  2 zucchini or yellow squash, cut into ½-inch slices
  1 small onion, cut into wedges
  1 small Japanese eggplant, cut into ½-inch slices
  2 red, green and/or yellow bell peppers, cut into chunks

In large resealable plastic bag, combine all ingredients; mix well. Seal bag and marinate in refrigerator at least 30 minutes. Remove vegetables; reserve used marinade. Grill or broil mixed vegetables 10 to 12 minutes or until tender (mushrooms cook quickly), turning once and brushing often with reserved marinade. Vegetables should be slightly "charred." Arrange vegetables on platter. *Makes 6 servings*

Variation: Place vegetables on skewers and grill over medium heat to desired doneness.

Hint: If oven roasting, preheat oven to 450°F. Vegetables should be slightly 'charred.' If roasting root vegetables, cover and roast 20 minutes. Uncover and continue roasting 20 to 25 minutes, or until tender.

tip:

A great recipe to take along as a picnic side dish, to top a main-dish salad, to wrap up in a tortilla or to add to a sandwich. Can be made ahead and kept in refrigerator until ready to use. Serve warm, cold or at room temperature!

Grilled Vegetable Platter

Barbecued Corn with Three Savory Butters

12 ears corn, unhusked
Three Savory Butters (recipes follow)

Carefully peel back husks; remove corn silk. Bring husks up and tie securely with kitchen string. Soak corn in cold water to cover 30 minutes. Place corn on grid. Grill over medium-hot coals 25 minutes or until corn is tender, turning often. Remove string and husks. Serve with your choice of Savory Butter. *Makes 12 side-dish servings*

Three Savory Butters

HORSERADISH BUTTER
½ **cup (1 stick) butter or margarine, softened**
3 **tablespoons** *French's*® **Bold 'n Spicy Brown Mustard**
1 **tablespoon horseradish**

CHILI BUTTER
½ **cup (1 stick) butter or margarine, softened**
2 **tablespoons** *Frank's*® *RedHot*® **Original Cayenne Pepper Sauce**
1 **teaspoon chili powder**
1 **clove garlic, minced**

HERB BUTTER
½ **cup (1 stick) butter or margarine, softened**
2 **tablespoons snipped fresh chives**
1 **tablespoon** *French's*® **Worcestershire Sauce**
1 **tablespoon minced fresh parsley**
½ **teaspoon dried thyme leaves**

Place ingredients for each flavored butter in separate small bowls; beat until smooth. Serve at room temperature. *Makes about ½ cup each*

Barbecued Corn with
Three Savory Butters

Eggplant Pasta Bake

Prep and Cook Time: 30 minutes

    4 ounces dry bow-tie pasta
    1 pound eggplant, diced
    1 clove garlic, minced
  ¼ cup olive oil
 1½ cups shredded Monterey Jack cheese, divided
    1 cup sliced green onions
  ½ cup grated Parmesan cheese
    1 can (14½ ounces) DEL MONTE® Diced Tomatoes with Basil, Garlic & Oregano, undrained

1. Preheat oven to 350°F. Cook pasta according to package directions; drain.

2. Cook eggplant and garlic in oil in large skillet over medium-high heat until tender.

3. Toss eggplant with cooked pasta, 1 cup Jack cheese, green onions and Parmesan cheese.

4. Place in greased 9-inch square baking dish. Top with undrained tomatoes and remaining ½ cup Jack cheese. Bake 15 minutes or until heated through.

Makes 6 servings

Double Mushroom Stuffing

   3 tablespoons I CAN'T BELIEVE IT'S NOT BUTTER!® Spread
   ½ cup chopped onion
   2 cups sliced white and shiitake mushrooms
2½ cups fresh ½-inch Italian or French bread cubes
   1 can (14½ ounces) chicken broth
   2 tablespoons chopped fresh parsley

In 12-inch nonstick skillet, melt I Can't Believe It's Not Butter!® Spread over medium-high heat and cook onion, stirring occasionally, 2 minutes or until softened. Add mushrooms and cook, stirring occasionally, 4 minutes or until golden. Stir in bread, ¾ cup broth (reserve remaining broth) and parsley. Season, if desired, with salt and ground black pepper. Spoon into greased 1-quart casserole.

During last 30 minutes of roasting, place stuffing casserole in oven with Cornish hens (page 142). Cook until stuffing is heated through and golden.   *Makes 2 servings*

Roasted Garlic Mashed Potatoes

   3 pounds all-purpose potatoes, peeled, if desired, and cut into chunks
   1 jar (1 pound) RAGÚ® Cheesy!® Roasted Garlic Parmesan Sauce
   ¼ cup chopped fresh parsley (optional)
   ½ teaspoon salt
   ¼ teaspoon ground black pepper

In 3-quart saucepan, cover potatoes with water. Bring to a boil over high heat. Reduce heat to low and simmer, uncovered, 20 minutes or until potatoes are very tender; drain. Return potatoes to saucepan; mash potatoes with Ragú Cheesy! Sauce, parsley, salt and pepper.
          Makes 12 servings

Sautéed Garlic Potatoes

2 pounds boiling potatoes, peeled and cut into 1-inch pieces

3 tablespoons FILIPPO BERIO® Olive Oil

6 cloves garlic, skins on

1 tablespoon lemon juice

1 tablespoon chopped fresh chives

1 tablespoon chopped fresh parsley

Salt and freshly ground black pepper

Place potatoes in large colander; rinse under cold running water. Drain well; pat dry. In large nonstick skillet, heat olive oil over medium heat until hot. Add potatoes in a single layer. Cook, stirring and turning frequently, 10 minutes or until golden brown. Add garlic. Cover; reduce heat to low and cook very gently, shaking pan and stirring mixture occasionally, 15 to 20 minutes or until potatoes are tender when pierced with fork. Remove garlic; remove and discard skins. In small bowl, crush garlic; stir in lemon juice. Add to potatoes; mix well. Cook 1 to 2 minutes or until heated through. Transfer to serving dish; sprinkle with chives and parsley. Season to taste with salt and pepper. *Makes 4 servings*

Baked Squash

2 medium-sized acorn squash

2 tart red apples, diced

½ cup chopped nuts

½ cup SMUCKER'S® Apple Jelly

¼ cup (½ stick) butter or margarine, softened

Cut squash in half crosswise or lengthwise; scoop out centers. Place in baking pan. Combine apples, nuts, jelly and butter. Fill squash with mixture. Pour a small amount of boiling water in bottom of pan around squash. Cover pan with foil.

Bake at 400°F for 45 to 60 minutes or until fork-tender. Remove foil during last 5 minutes of baking. *Makes 4 servings*

Sautéed Garlic Potatoes

Acorn Squash Filled with Savory Spinach

4 small acorn squash

2 tablespoons FILIPPO BERIO® Olive Oil

1 (10-ounce) package frozen chopped spinach, thawed and drained

1 (8-ounce) container ricotta cheese

1 tablespoon grated Parmesan cheese

¼ teaspoon freshly ground black pepper

⅛ teaspoon salt

⅛ teaspoon ground nutmeg

Preheat oven to 325°F. Cut squash crosswise in half. Scoop out seeds and fibers; discard. Brush insides and outsides of squash halves with olive oil. Place in large shallow roasting pan. Bake, uncovered, 35 to 40 minutes or until tender when pierced with fork.

In medium bowl, combine spinach, ricotta cheese, Parmesan cheese, pepper, salt and nutmeg. Spoon equal amounts of spinach mixture into squash halves. Bake, uncovered, an additional 10 to 15 minutes or until heated through. *Makes 8 servings*

To Microwave: Prepare squash as directed above. Place in large shallow microwave-safe dish. Cover with vented plastic wrap. Microwave on HIGH (100% power) 10 to 12 minutes or until squash are softened, rotating dish halfway through cooking. Prepare filling; spoon into squash halves. Cover with vented plastic wrap; microwave on HIGH 6 to 8 minutes or until filling is hot and squash are tender when pierced with fork.

Acorn Squash Filled with Savory Spinach

Double Cheddar Bacon Mashed Potatoes

Prep Time: 10 minutes
Cook Time: 20 minutes

> **2 pounds all-purpose potatoes, peeled and sliced**
> **1 jar (1 pound) RAGÚ® Cheesy!® Double Cheddar Sauce, heated**
> **5 slices bacon, crisp-cooked and crumbled (about ¼ cup)**
> **1 teaspoon salt**

1. In 3-quart saucepan, cover potatoes with water. Bring to a boil over high heat. Reduce heat to low and simmer uncovered 15 minutes or until potatoes are very tender; drain. Return potatoes to saucepan. Mash potatoes.

2. Stir Ragú Cheesy! Sauce into mashed potatoes. Stir in bacon and salt.

Makes 6 servings

Diner Skillet Potatoes

> **3 pounds all-purpose potatoes, peeled and diced**
> **2 large red or green bell peppers, chopped**
> **1 envelope LIPTON® RECIPE SECRETS® Onion Soup Mix**
> **2 tablespoons BERTOLLI® Olive Oil**

1. In large bowl, combine potatoes, red peppers and Onion Soup Mix until evenly coated.

2. In 12-inch nonstick skillet, heat oil over medium heat and cook potato mixture, covered, stirring occasionally, 12 minutes. Remove cover and continue cooking, stirring occasionally, 10 minutes or until potatoes are tender. *Makes about 6 servings*

Oven-Roasted Vegetables

**1 envelope LIPTON® RECIPE SECRETS® Savory Herb
    with Garlic Soup Mix***

1½ pounds assorted fresh vegetables**

2 tablespoons BERTOLLI® Olive Oil

**Also terrific with LIPTON® RECIPE SECRETS® Onion or Golden
Onion Soup Mix.*

***Use any combination of the following, sliced: zucchini; yellow squash; red, green or yellow bell
peppers; carrots; celery and/or mushrooms.*

1. Preheat oven to 450°F. In large plastic bag or bowl, combine all ingredients. Close bag
and shake, or toss in bowl, until vegetables are evenly coated.

2. In 13×9-inch baking or roasting pan, arrange vegetables; discard bag.

3. Bake uncovered, stirring once, 20 minutes or until vegetables are tender.

Makes 4 servings

Microwave Sweet Potato Chips

2 cups thinly sliced sweet potatoes

1 tablespoon packed brown sugar

2 teaspoons margarine

MICROWAVE DIRECTIONS
Place sweet potatoes in single layer in microwavable dish. Sprinkle with water. Microwave
at HIGH 5 minutes. Stir in brown sugar and margarine. Microwave at HIGH 2 to 3 minutes.
Let stand a few minutes before serving.

Makes 4 servings

Favorite recipe from **The Sugar Association, Inc.**

Green Beans with Toasted Pecans

    3 tablespoons I CAN'T BELIEVE IT'S NOT BUTTER!® Spread, melted

    1 teaspoon sugar

    ¼ teaspoon LAWRY'S® Garlic Powder with Parsley

      Pinch ground red pepper

      Salt to taste

    ⅓ cup chopped pecans

    1 pound green beans

In small bowl, blend I Can't Believe It's Not Butter!® Spread, sugar, garlic powder, pepper and salt.

In 12-inch nonstick skillet, heat 2 teaspoons garlic mixture over medium-high heat and cook pecans, stirring frequently, 2 minutes or until pecans are golden. Remove pecans and set aside.

In same skillet, heat remaining garlic mixture and stir in green beans. Cook, covered, over medium heat, stirring occasionally, 6 minutes or until green beans are tender. Stir in pecans.
Makes 4 servings

Oven-Roasted Asparagus

    1 pound asparagus

    2 tablespoons I CAN'T BELIEVE IT'S NOT BUTTER!® Spread, melted

    2 cloves garlic, finely chopped

      Salt and ground black pepper to taste

Preheat oven to 425°F.

In large bowl, combine all ingredients. In 1½-quart baking dish, arrange asparagus mixture. Roast 20 minutes or until asparagus are tender. Garnish, if desired, with grated lemon peel and serve with lemon wedges.
Makes 4 servings

Note: Recipe can be halved.

Green Beans with Toasted Pecans

Roasted Idaho & Sweet Potatoes

1 envelope LIPTON® RECIPE SECRETS® Onion Soup Mix

2 medium all-purpose potatoes, peeled, if desired, and cut into large chunks (about 1 pound)

2 medium sweet potatoes or yams, peeled, if desired, and cut into large chunks (about 1 pound)

¼ cup BERTOLLI® Olive Oil

1. Preheat oven to 425°F. In large plastic bag or bowl, combine all ingredients. Close bag and shake, or toss in bowl, until potatoes are evenly coated.

2. In 13×9-inch baking or roasting pan, arrange potatoes; discard bag.

3. Bake uncovered, stirring occasionally, 40 minutes or until potatoes are tender and golden.

Makes 4 servings

Alouette® Artichokes

1 (6.5-ounce) package ALOUETTE® Garlic & Herbs

2 (13-ounce) cans artichoke hearts

¼ cup bread crumbs

Fresh chervil or parsley

Preheat oven to 350°F.

With thumb, make an impression in each artichoke heart. Fill each artichoke with 1 teaspoon Alouette and sprinkle with bread crumbs.

Place in baking pan; bake 15 minutes.

Place under broiler until bread crumbs are slightly browned. Garnish with fresh chervil.

Makes 6 servings

Roasted Idaho & Sweet Potatoes

Zippy Oven Fries

Prep Time: 10 minutes
Cook Time: 25 minutes

   1 pound russet potatoes, sliced into ¼-inch wedges
   3 tablespoons butter or vegetable oil
   2 tablespoons *Frank's® RedHot®* Original Cayenne Pepper
      Sauce, at room temperature
   2 cups *French's®* French Fried Onions, finely crushed
  ½ cup grated Parmesan cheese
    Zestup Ketchup (recipe follows)

1. Preheat oven to 400°F. Place potatoes, butter and *Frank's RedHot* Sauce in large resealable plastic bag. Seal bag and toss potatoes to coat.

2. Combine French Fried Onions and cheese on sheet of waxed paper. Coat potatoes in crumb mixture, pressing firmly.

3. Arrange potatoes in single layer in shallow baking pan coated with nonstick cooking spray. Bake, uncovered, 25 minutes or until potatoes are tender and golden brown. Splash on more *Frank's RedHot* Sauce or serve with Zestup Ketchup.   *Makes 4 servings*

Zestup Ketchup: Combine 1 cup ketchup with 1 to 2 tablespoons *Frank's RedHot* Sauce.

Marinated Mushrooms

2 pounds mushrooms
1 bottle (8 ounces) Italian salad dressing
   Grated peel of ½ SUNKIST® lemon
   Juice of 1 SUNKIST® lemon
2 tablespoons sliced pimiento (optional)
2 tablespoons chopped fresh parsley

In large saucepan, combine mushrooms and Italian dressing; bring to a boil. Cook, uncovered, 2 to 3 minutes, stirring constantly. Add lemon peel, juice and pimiento. Chill 4 hours or more. Drain, reserving dressing for another use. Stir parsley into mushrooms. Garnish with lemon cartwheel slices, if desired.   *Makes about 4 cups*

Note: Reserved dressing may be used on salads. Makes about 1½ cups.

Grilled Asparagus

1 pound fresh asparagus
   CRISCO® No-Stick Cooking Spray
½ teaspoon salt
¼ teaspoon freshly ground black pepper

1. Prepare charcoal or gas grill. Trim woody stems off asparagus by breaking stalks. Spray asparagus with CRISCO No-Stick Cooking Spray.

2. Grill asparagus for 3 minutes. Turn spears with tongs. Grill 3 to 4 minutes. Sprinkle with salt and pepper. Serve immediately.   *Makes 4 servings*

Twice Baked Potatoes

Prep Time: 10 minutes
Cook Time: 22 minutes

3 hot baked potatoes, split lengthwise
½ cup sour cream
2 tablespoons butter or margarine
1⅓ cups *French's*® French Fried Onions, divided
1 cup (4 ounces) shredded Cheddar cheese, divided
Dash paprika (optional)

1. Preheat oven to 400°F. Scoop out inside of potatoes into medium bowl, leaving thin shells. Mash potatoes with sour cream and butter until smooth. Stir in ⅔ *cup* French Fried Onions and ½ cup cheese. Spoon mixture into shells.

2. Bake 20 minutes or until heated through. Top with remaining cheese, onions and paprika, if desired. Bake 2 minutes or until cheese melts.   *Makes 6 servings*

Variation: For added Cheddar flavor, substitute *French's*® **Cheddar French Fried Onions** for the original flavor.

> ### tip:
> To bake potatoes quickly, microwave on HIGH 10 to 12 minutes or until tender.

Twice Baked Potatoes

Golden Corn Pudding

Prep Time: 10 minutes
Bake Time: 35 minutes

   2 tablespoons butter or margarine
   3 tablespoons all-purpose flour
   1 can (14¾ ounces) DEL MONTE® Cream Style Golden Sweet Corn
   ¼ cup yellow cornmeal
   2 eggs, separated
   1 package (3 ounces) cream cheese, softened
   1 can (8¾ ounces) DEL MONTE Whole Kernel Golden Sweet Corn, drained

1. Preheat oven to 350°F.

2. Melt butter in medium saucepan. Add flour and stir until smooth. Blend in cream style corn and cornmeal. Bring to a boil over medium heat, stirring constantly.

3. Place egg yolks in small bowl; stir in ½ cup hot mixture. Pour mixture back into saucepan. Add cream cheese and whole kernel corn.

4. Place egg whites in clean narrow bowl and beat until stiff peaks form. With rubber spatula, gently fold egg whites into corn mixture.

5. Pour mixture into 1½-quart straight-sided baking dish. Bake 30 to 35 minutes or until lightly browned.   *Makes 4 to 6 servings*

tip:

Pudding can be prepared up to 3 hours ahead of serving time. Cover and refrigerate until about 30 minutes before baking.

Creamy Spinach Italiano

Prep Time: 10 minutes
Cook Time: 35 minutes

> 1 cup ricotta cheese
> ¾ cup half-and-half or milk
> 2 packages (10 ounces each) frozen chopped spinach, thawed
> and squeezed dry
> 1⅓ cups *French's*® French Fried Onions, divided
> ½ cup chopped roasted red pepper
> ¼ cup chopped fresh basil
> ¼ cup grated Parmesan cheese
> 1 teaspoon garlic powder
> ¼ teaspoon salt

1. Preheat oven to 350°F. Whisk together ricotta cheese and half-and-half in large bowl until well combined. Stir in spinach, ⅔ *cup* French Fried Onions, red pepper, basil, Parmesan, garlic powder and salt. Pour mixture into greased deep-dish 9-inch pie plate.

2. Bake for 25 minutes or until heated through; stir. Sprinkle with remaining ⅔ *cup* onions. Bake for 5 minutes or until onions are golden. *Makes 4 servings*

Beef with Dry Spice Rub (page 130)

Grilled Chicken Croissant with Roasted Pepper Dressing (page 137)

main attractions

Awaken your taste buds with delicious entrées like Turkey Breast with Southwestern Corn Bread Dressing, Beef with Dry Spice Rub or Grilled Chicken Croissant with Roasted Pepper Dressing.

Turkey Breast with Southwestern Corn Bread Dressing (page 136)

Barbecued Salmon

4 salmon steaks, ¾ to 1 inch thick

3 tablespoons lemon juice

2 tablespoons soy sauce

Salt and black pepper

½ cup KC MASTERPIECE™ Original Barbecue Sauce

Fresh oregano sprigs

Grilled mushrooms (optional)

Rinse salmon; pat dry with paper towels. Combine lemon juice and soy sauce in shallow glass dish. Add salmon; let stand at cool room temperature no more than 15 to 20 minutes, turning salmon several times. Remove salmon from marinade; discard marinade. Season lightly with salt and pepper.

Lightly oil hot grid to prevent sticking. Grill salmon on covered grill over medium KINGSFORD® Briquets 10 to 14 minutes. Halfway through cooking time brush salmon with barbecue sauce, then turn and continue grilling until fish flakes when tested with fork. Remove fish from grill; brush with remaining barbecue sauce. Garnish with oregano sprigs and mushrooms.

Makes 4 servings

Ranch Crispy Chicken

¼ cup unseasoned dry bread crumbs or cornflake crumbs

1 packet (1 ounce) HIDDEN VALLEY® The Original Ranch® Salad Dressing & Seasoning Mix

6 bone-in chicken pieces

Combine bread crumbs and salad dressing & seasoning mix in a gallon-size Glad® Zipper Storage Bag. Add chicken pieces; seal bag. Shake to coat chicken. Bake chicken on ungreased baking pan at 375°F for 50 minutes or until no longer pink in center and juices run clear.

Makes 4 to 6 servings

Barbecued Salmon

Napa Valley Chicken Salad

2 cups diced cooked chicken

1 cup seedless red grapes, halved

1 cup diced celery

½ cup chopped toasted pecans

¼ cup thinly sliced green onions

½ cup HIDDEN VALLEY® The Original Ranch® Salad Dressing

1 teaspoon Dijon mustard

Combine chicken, grapes, celery, pecans and onions in a medium bowl. Stir together dressing and mustard; toss with salad. Cover and refrigerate for 2 hours. *Makes 4 servings*

Beef with Dry Spice Rub

3 tablespoons firmly packed brown sugar

1 tablespoon yellow mustard seeds

1 tablespoon whole coriander seeds

1 tablespoon black peppercorns

4 cloves garlic

1½ to 2 pounds beef top round (London Broil) steak, about 1½ inches thick

Vegetable or olive oil

Salt

Place sugar, mustard seeds, coriander seeds, peppercorns and garlic in blender or food processor; process until seeds and garlic are crushed. Rub beef with oil; pat on spice mixture. Season generously with salt.

Lightly oil hot grid to prevent sticking. Grill beef, on covered grill, over medium-low KINGSFORD® Briquets 16 to 20 minutes for medium rare or until desired doneness, turning once. Let stand 5 minutes before cutting across the grain into thin diagonal slices.

Makes 6 servings

Napa Valley Chicken Salad

Country Glazed Ribs

Prep Time: 10 minutes
Marinate Time: 1 hour
Cook Time: 45 minutes

> 3 to 4 pounds pork baby back ribs, cut into 3- to 4-rib portions
> ½ cup *French's*® Bold 'n Spicy Brown Mustard
> ½ cup packed brown sugar
> ½ cup finely chopped onion
> ¼ cup *French's*® Worcestershire Sauce
> ¼ cup cider vinegar
> 1 tablespoon mustard seeds
> 1 teaspoon ground allspice
> Honey Mustard Dip (recipe follows)

Place ribs in large shallow glass baking pan or resealable plastic food storage bag. To prepare marinade, combine mustard, sugar, onion, Worcestershire, vinegar, mustard seeds and allspice in small bowl; mix well. Pour over ribs, turning to coat all sides. Cover and marinate in refrigerator 1 hour or overnight.

Place ribs on grid, reserving marinade. Grill over medium coals 45 minutes or until ribs are barely pink near bone, turning and basting frequently with marinade. (Do not baste during last 10 minutes of cooking.) Serve with Honey Mustard Dip. Garnish as desired.

Makes 4 to 6 servings

Honey Mustard Dip

> ½ cup *French's*® Bold 'n Spicy Brown Mustard
> ½ cup honey

Combine mustard and honey in small bowl; mix well.

Makes 1 cup

Country Glazed Ribs

BBQ Pork Sandwiches

Prep Time: 10 minutes
Cook Time: 5 hours

4 pounds boneless pork loin roast, fat trimmed
1 can (14½ ounces) beef broth
⅓ cup *French's*® Worcestershire Sauce
⅓ cup *Frank's*® *RedHot*® Original Cayenne Pepper Sauce

SAUCE

½ cup ketchup
½ cup molasses
¼ cup *French's*® Classic Yellow® Mustard
¼ cup *French's*® Worcestershire Sauce
2 tablespoons *Frank's*® *RedHot*® Original Cayenne Pepper Sauce

SLOW COOKER DIRECTIONS

1. Place roast on bottom of slow cooker. Combine broth, *⅓ cup each* Worcestershire and **Frank's RedHot** Sauce. Pour over roast. Cover and cook on high-heat setting 5 hours* or until roast is tender.

2. Meanwhile, combine ingredients for sauce in large bowl; set aside.

3. Transfer roast to large cutting board. Discard liquid. Coarsely chop roast. Stir into reserved sauce. Spoon pork mixture on large rolls. Serve with deli potato salad, if desired.

Makes 8 to 10 servings

Or cook 10 hours on low-heat setting.

tip:

Make additional sauce and serve on the side.
Great also with barbecued ribs and chops!

BBQ Pork Sandwich

Turkey Breast with Southwestern Corn Bread Dressing

    5 cups coarsely crumbled prepared corn bread

    4 English muffins, coarsely crumbled

    3 Anaheim chilies,* roasted, peeled, seeded and chopped

    1 red bell pepper, roasted, peeled, seeded and chopped

    ¾ cup pine nuts, toasted

    1 tablespoon *each* chopped fresh cilantro and chopped
        fresh parsley

    1½ teaspoons chopped fresh basil *or* ½ teaspoon dried basil leaves

    1½ teaspoons chopped fresh thyme *or* ½ teaspoon dried thyme leaves

    1½ teaspoons chopped fresh oregano *or* ½ teaspoon dried oregano leaves

    1 pound Italian turkey sausage

    3 cups chopped celery

    1 cup chopped onions

    2 to 4 tablespoons chicken or turkey broth

    1 bone-in turkey breast (5 to 6 pounds)

    2 tablespoons minced garlic

    ½ cup chopped fresh cilantro

    Red and green whole peppers, for garnish

Anaheim chilies can sting and irritate the skin; wear rubber gloves when handling peppers and do not touch eyes. Wash hands after handling.

1. Preheat oven to 325°F. In large bowl combine corn bread, muffins, chilies, bell pepper, pine nuts, 1 tablespoon cilantro, parsley, basil, thyme and oregano; set aside.

2. In large skillet, over medium-high heat, cook and stir turkey sausage, celery and onions 8 to 10 minutes or until sausage is no longer pink and vegetables are tender. Add to corn bread mixture. Add broth if mixture is too dry; set aside.

3. Loosen skin on both sides of turkey breast, being careful not to tear skin, leaving it connected at breast bone. Spread 1 tablespoon garlic under loosened skin over each breast half. Repeat procedure, spreading ¼ cup cilantro over each breast half.

4. Place turkey breast on rack in 13×9×2-inch roasting pan lightly coated with nonstick cooking spray. Spoon half of stuffing mixture under breast cavity. Spoon remaining stuffing into 2-quart casserole lightly coated with nonstick cooking spray. Cover and refrigerate.

5. Roast turkey breast, uncovered, 2 to 2½ hours or until meat thermometer registers 170°F in deepest portion of breast. Bake remaining stuffing, uncovered, during last 45 minutes.

6. Allow turkey breast to stand for 15 minutes before carving. Transfer to platter and garnish with red and green whole peppers.   *Makes 12 servings*

Favorite recipe from **National Turkey Federation**

Grilled Chicken Croissant with Roasted Pepper Dressing

Prep Time: 15 minutes
Cook Time: 15 minutes

    ½ cup *French's*® Honey Dijon Mustard
    3 tablespoons *each* olive oil and red wine vinegar
    ¾ teaspoon *each* Italian seasoning and garlic powder
    1 jar (7 ounces) roasted red peppers, drained
    1 pound boneless skinless chicken breast halves
        Lettuce leaves
    4 croissants, split

Whisk together mustard, oil, vinegar, Italian seasoning and garlic powder in small bowl until well blended. Pour ¼ cup mixture into blender. Add peppers. Cover and process until mixture is smooth; set aside.

Brush chicken pieces with remaining mustard mixture. Place pieces on grid. Grill over hot coals 15 minutes or until chicken is no longer pink in center, turning often. To serve, place lettuce leaves on bottom halves of croissants. Arrange chicken on top of lettuce. Spoon roasted pepper dressing over chicken. Cover with croissant top. Garnish as desired.

Makes 4 servings

Pork & Rice Provençal

Prep Time: 10 minutes
Cook Time: 40 minutes

  4 well-trimmed boneless pork loin chops, ¾-inch thick (about 1 pound)
  1 teaspoon dried basil
  ½ teaspoon dried thyme
  ½ teaspoon garlic salt
  ¼ teaspoon ground black pepper
  2 tablespoons margarine or butter, divided
  1 (6.8-ounce) package RICE-A-RONI® Beef Flavor
  ½ cup chopped onion
  1 clove garlic, minced
  1 (14½-ounce) can seasoned diced tomatoes, undrained
  1 (2¼-ounce) can sliced ripe olives, drained *or* ⅓ cup sliced pitted kalamata olives

1. Sprinkle pork chops with basil, thyme, garlic salt and pepper; set aside. In large skillet over medium-high heat, melt 1 tablespoon margarine. Add pork chops; cook 3 minutes. Reduce heat to medium; turn pork chops over and cook 3 minutes. Remove from skillet; set aside.

2. In same skillet over medium heat, sauté rice-vermicelli mix, onion and garlic with remaining 1 tablespoon margarine until vermicelli is golden brown.

3. Slowly stir in 1¾ cups water, tomatoes and Special Seasonings; bring to a boil. Cover; reduce heat to low. Simmer 10 minutes.

4. Add pork chops and olives. Cover; simmer 10 minutes or until rice is tender and pork chops are no longer pink inside. *Makes 4 servings*

Pork & Rice Provençal

Baked Salmon in Foil

2 tablespoons FILIPPO BERIO® Olive Oil, divided
1 (10-ounce) package frozen chopped spinach, thawed and squeezed dry
1 (8-ounce) can stewed tomatoes
1 onion, chopped
1 clove garlic, minced
4 salmon steaks, 1 inch thick (about 2 pounds)
4 pieces heavy-duty aluminum foil, each cut into a 12-inch square
4 thin lemon slices
1 tablespoon coarsely chopped fresh parsley
  Salt and freshly ground black pepper

Preheat oven to 375°F. In medium saucepan, heat 1 tablespoon olive oil over medium heat until hot. Add spinach, tomatoes, onion and garlic. Cook, stirring occasionally, 5 minutes or until mixture is thick and onion is tender.

In medium skillet, heat remaining 1 tablespoon olive oil over medium-high heat until hot. Add salmon; cook 1 to 2 minutes on each side or until lightly browned. Remove from heat. Place one-fourth of spinach mixture in center of each piece of foil; top with one salmon steak. Drizzle liquid from skillet over salmon. Top each with lemon slice and parsley. Fold edges of each foil square together. Pinch well to seal, completely enclosing filling. Place on baking sheet. Bake 15 minutes or until salmon flakes easily when tested with fork. To serve, cut an "X" in top of each packet; carefully peel back foil. Season to taste with salt and pepper.

Makes 4 servings

Baked Salmon in Foil

Roasted Cornish Hens with Double Mushroom Stuffing

2 Cornish hens (about 1½ pounds each)

½ teaspoon salt

¼ teaspoon ground black pepper

3 tablespoons I CAN'T BELIEVE IT'S NOT BUTTER!® Spread

1 tablespoon finely chopped shallot or onion

2 teaspoons chopped fresh tarragon leaves or ½ teaspoon dried tarragon leaves, crushed (optional)

½ lemon, cut in 2 wedges

Double Mushroom Stuffing (page 109)

1 tablespoon all-purpose flour

Preheat oven to 425°F. Season hens and hen cavities with salt and pepper.

In small bowl, blend I Can't Believe It's Not Butter!® Spread, shallot and tarragon; evenly spread under skin. Place 1 lemon wedge in each hen.

In 18×12-inch roasting pan, on rack, arrange hens breast side up; tie legs together with string. Roast uncovered 15 minutes.

Meanwhile, prepare Double Mushroom Stuffing.

Decrease heat to 350°F and place Double Mushroom Stuffing casserole in oven with hens. Continue roasting hens 30 minutes or until meat thermometer inserted in thickest part of thigh reaches 180°F and stuffing is golden. Remove hens to serving platter and keep warm. Remove rack from pan.

Skim fat from pan drippings. Blend flour with reserved broth from stuffing; stir into pan drippings. Place roasting pan over heat and bring to a boil over high heat, stirring frequently. Reduce heat to low and simmer, stirring occasionally, 1 minute or until gravy is thickened. Serve gravy and stuffing with hens. *Makes 2 servings*

Four-Cheese Lasagna

Prep Time: 1½ hours

  ½ **pound ground beef**

  ½ **cup chopped onion**

  ⅓ **cup chopped celery**

  1 **clove garlic, minced**

1½ **teaspoons dried basil leaves**

  ¼ **teaspoon dried oregano leaves**

  ¼ **teaspoon salt**

  ⅛ **teaspoon ground black pepper**

  1 **package (3 ounces) cream cheese, cubed**

  ⅓ **cup light cream or milk**

  ½ **cup dry white wine**

  ½ **cup (2 ounces) shredded Wisconsin Cheddar or Gouda cheese**

  1 **egg, slightly beaten**

  1 **cup cream-style cottage cheese**

  6 **ounces lasagna noodles, cooked and drained**

  6 **ounces sliced Wisconsin Mozzarella cheese**

In large skillet, brown meat with onion, celery and garlic; drain. Stir in basil, oregano, salt and pepper. Reduce heat to low. Add cream cheese and cream. Cook, stirring frequently, until cream cheese is melted. Stir in wine. Gradually add Cheddar cheese, stirring until Cheddar cheese is almost melted. Remove from heat. In small bowl, combine egg and cottage cheese.

In greased 10×6-inch baking dish, layer ½ each of the noodles, meat sauce, cottage cheese mixture and Mozzarella cheese; repeat layers. Bake, uncovered, at 375°F, 30 to 35 minutes or until hot and bubbly. Let stand 10 minutes before cutting to serve. *Makes 6 servings*

Favorite recipe from **Wisconsin Milk Marketing Board**

Oriental Flank Steak

Prep Time: 5 minutes
Cook Time: 15 minutes
Marinate Time: 3 hours

¾ **cup WISH-BONE® Italian Dressing***
3 **tablespoons soy sauce**
3 **tablespoons firmly packed brown sugar**
½ **teaspoon ground ginger (optional)**
1 **to 1½ pounds flank, top round or sirloin steak**

Also terrific with Wish-Bone® Robusto Italian, Lite Italian or Red Wine Vinaigrette Dressing.

In small bowl, combine all ingredients except steak.

In large, shallow nonaluminum baking dish or plastic bag, pour ½ cup marinade over steak. Cover, or close bag, and marinate in refrigerator, turning occasionally, 3 to 24 hours. Refrigerate remaining marinade.

Remove steak from marinade, discarding marinade. Grill or broil steak, turning once and brushing frequently with reserved marinade until steak is desired doneness.

Makes about 4 servings

Oriental Flank Steak

Cheese-Stuffed Meat Loaf

Prep Time: 20 minutes
Cook Time: 1 hour

1½ pounds ground beef
1 jar (1 pound 10 ounces) RAGÚ® Chunky Pasta Sauce, divided
1 egg, lightly beaten
¼ cup plain dry bread crumbs
2 cups (about 8 ounces) shredded mozzarella cheese
1 tablespoon finely chopped fresh parsley

1. Preheat oven to 350°F. In large bowl, combine ground beef, ⅓ cup Ragú Pasta Sauce, egg and bread crumbs. Season, if desired, with salt and ground black pepper. In 13×9-inch baking or roasting pan, shape meat mixture into 12×8-inch rectangle.

2. Sprinkle 1½ cups cheese and parsley down center of meat loaf leaving ¾-inch border. Roll, starting at long end, jelly-roll style. Press ends together to seal.

3. Bake uncovered 45 minutes. Pour remaining sauce over meat loaf and sprinkle with remaining ½ cup cheese. Bake an additional 15 minutes or until sauce is heated through and cheese is melted. Let stand 5 minutes before serving.   *Makes 6 servings*

tip:

Molding the meat mixture on waxed paper helps make rolling easier. Just lift waxed paper to curl the meat over cheese filling, then carefully remove meat from paper. Continue rolling until filling is enclosed in roll and meat is off paper.

Cheese-Stuffed Meat Loaf

Snappy Pea and Chicken Pot Pie

2½ cups chicken broth

  1 medium-size baking potato, peeled and cut into ½-inch chunks

1½ cups (½-inch slices) carrot

  1 cup frozen pearl onions

  ½ teaspoon dried rosemary

  ½ teaspoon TABASCO® brand Pepper Sauce

  ¼ teaspoon salt

  1 medium red bell pepper, coarsely diced

  4 ounces (about 1 cup) sugar-snap peas, trimmed and halved lengthwise

  3 tablespoons butter or margarine

  ¼ cup flour

  8 ounces cooked chicken-breast meat, cut in 3×1-inch strips

  1 sheet frozen puff pastry, thawed

  1 egg, beaten with 1 teaspoon water

In large heavy saucepan bring chicken broth to a boil over high heat. Add potato, carrots, onions, rosemary, TABASCO® Sauce and salt. Reduce heat to medium; cover and simmer 8 to 10 minutes, until vegetables are tender. Add bell pepper and sugar-snap peas; boil 30 seconds, just until peas turn bright green. Drain vegetables, reserving chicken broth; set aside.

Melt butter in saucepan over low heat. Stir in flour; cook 3 to 4 minutes, stirring constantly. Pour in 2 cups of reserved chicken broth; whisk until smooth. Bring to a boil over medium heat, stirring constantly. Reduce heat to low; simmer 5 minutes, stirring frequently, until thickened and bubbly.

Put chicken strips in bottoms of four lightly buttered ramekins. Top chicken with vegetables and sauce. Heat oven to 475°F.

Unfold puff pastry on floured surface according to package directions. Cut pastry into four rectangles. Brush outside rims of ramekins with some of the beaten egg mixture. Place pastry rectangle over each ramekin and press firmly around edges to seal. Trim dough and flute edges. Brush tops with remaining beaten egg mixture.

Place ramekins on baking sheet and bake 10 to 12 minutes, until pastry is puffed and well browned. Serve at once.

Makes 4 servings

Sloppy Joes

  1 pound lean ground beef or turkey
½ cup chopped onion
⅓ cup chopped green bell pepper
  1 bottle (12 ounces) HEINZ® Chili Sauce
¼ cup water
  1 to 2 tablespoons brown sugar
  1 tablespoon HEINZ® Worcestershire Sauce
¼ teaspoon salt
⅛ teaspoon black pepper
    Sandwich buns

In large saucepan, cook beef, onion and bell pepper until pepper is tender; drain, if necessary. Stir in Chili Sauce, water, sugar, Worcestershire sauce, salt and black pepper; simmer 10 minutes, stirring occasionally. Serve in sandwich buns.   *Makes 6 to 8 servings*

Balsamic Chicken Salad

Prep Time: 10 minutes

  ⅓ cup olive oil
¼ cup *French's*® Sweet & Tangy Honey Mustard
  2 tablespoons balsamic or red wine vinegar
  1 teaspoon minced shallots or onion
  8 cups mixed salad greens, washed and torn
  1 package (10 ounces) fully cooked carved chicken breasts
  1 package (4 ounces) goat or Feta cheese, crumbled
  1 cup croutons

1. Whisk together oil, mustard, vinegar, shallots, *2 tablespoons water* and *⅛ teaspoon salt*.

2. Arrange salad greens, chicken, cheese and croutons on serving plates. Serve with dressing.
Makes 4 servings

Steak Provençal

　4 beef ribeye, sirloin or tenderloin steaks (about 11 ounces each)
　5 tablespoons I CAN'T BELIEVE IT'S NOT BUTTER!® Spread
　2 large cloves garlic, finely chopped
1½ cups chopped tomatoes (about 2 medium)
　1 to 2 tablespoons rinsed and chopped large capers
　¼ teaspoon salt
　¼ teaspoon ground black pepper
　2 tablespoons chopped fresh parsley

Grill or broil steaks to desired doneness.

Meanwhile, in 10-inch skillet, melt I Can't Believe It's Not Butter!® Spread and cook garlic over medium heat, stirring occasionally, 30 seconds. Add tomatoes, capers, salt and pepper. Cook, stirring occasionally, 3 minutes or until tomatoes are cooked and mixture is saucy. Stir in parsley. Serve over hot steaks.　　　　　　　　　　　　　*Makes 4 servings*

Crispy Garlic Chicken

　1 envelope LIPTON® RECIPE SECRETS® Savory Herb with Garlic Soup Mix*
　⅓ cup HELLMANN'S® or BEST FOODS® Real Mayonnaise
　¼ cup grated Parmesan cheese
　6 boneless, skinless chicken breast halves (about 1¾ pounds)
　2 tablespoons plain dry bread crumbs

Also terrific with LIPTON® RECIPE SECRETS® Onion Soup Mix.

1. Preheat oven to 400°F. In medium bowl, combine soup mix, mayonnaise and cheese; set aside.

2. On baking sheet, arrange chicken. Evenly top chicken with soup mixture, then evenly sprinkle with bread crumbs.

3. Bake 20 minutes or until chicken is thoroughly cooked.　　　　　*Makes 6 servings*

Steak Provençal

Lipton® Onion Burgers

Prep Time: 10 minutes
Cook Time: 12 minutes

> 1 envelope LIPTON® RECIPE SECRETS® Onion Soup Mix*
> 2 pounds ground beef
> ½ cup water

Also terrific with LIPTON® RECIPE SECRETS® Beefy Onion, Onion Mushroom, Beefy Mushroom, Savory Herb with Garlic or Ranch Soup Mix.

1. In large bowl, combine all ingredients; shape into 8 patties.

2. Grill or broil until done.

Makes 8 servings

Roasted Chicken au Jus

> 1 envelope LIPTON® RECIPE SECRETS® Onion Soup Mix*
> 2 tablespoons BERTOLLI® Olive Oil
> 1 (2½- to 3-pound) chicken, cut into serving pieces
> ½ cup hot water

Also terrific with LIPTON® RECIPE SECRETS® Savory Herb with Garlic or Onion Mushroom Soup Mix.

1. Preheat oven to 425°F. In large bowl, combine soup mix and oil; add chicken and toss until evenly coated.

2. In bottom of broiler pan without rack, arrange chicken. Roast chicken, basting occasionally, 40 minutes or until chicken is thoroughly cooked.

3. Remove chicken to serving platter. Add hot water to pan and stir, scraping brown bits from bottom of pan. Serve sauce over chicken.

Makes 4 servings

Slow Cooker Method: Rub chicken pieces with soup mix combined with oil. Place chicken in slow cooker. Cover. Cook on HIGH 4 hours or LOW 6 to 8 hours. Serve as above.

Lipton® Onion Burgers

Super Pork Burger

Prep Time: 15 minutes
Cook Time: 15 minutes

> 1 (8-ounce) can crushed pineapple
> ¾ **pound fully cooked boneless smoked ham**
> ¾ **pound ground pork**
> ½ **cup finely chopped green bell pepper**
> 2 **tablespoons all-purpose flour**
> ¼ **teaspoon ground allspice**

Drain pineapple, reserving juice.

Coarsely chop ham. Place ham in food processor bowl; process about 30 seconds or until coarsely ground.

In mixing bowl combine pineapple, ground ham, ground pork, bell pepper, flour and allspice; mix well. Shape into six ½-inch-thick patties. Place patties on unheated rack in broiler pan. Broil 6 inches from heat about 8 minutes.

Meanwhile, in small saucepan cook pineapple juice over medium heat until reduced by half. Brush patties with half of pineapple juice; turn and broil 6 minutes longer. Brush patties with remaining pineapple juice.   *Makes 6 servings*

Favorite recipe from **National Pork Board**

Super Pork Burger

Peppered Steak with Dijon Sauce

Prep Time: 10 minutes
Cook Time: 15 minutes

  4 boneless beef top loin (New York strip) steaks, cut 1 inch thick (about 1½ pounds)
  1 tablespoon *French's* Worcestershire Sauce
    Crushed black pepper
  ⅓ cup mayonnaise
  ⅓ cup *French's* Honey Dijon Mustard
  3 tablespoons dry red wine
  2 tablespoons minced red or green onion
  2 tablespoons minced fresh parsley
  1 clove garlic, minced

1. Brush steaks with Worcestershire and sprinkle with pepper to taste; set aside. To prepare Dijon sauce, combine mayonnaise, mustard, wine, onion, parsley and garlic in medium bowl.

2. Place steaks on grid. Grill steaks over high heat 15 minutes for medium rare or to desired doneness, turning often. Serve with Dijon sauce. Garnish as desired.   *Makes 4 servings*

tip:

Dijon sauce is also great served with grilled salmon and swordfish. To serve with fish, substitute white wine for red wine and minced dill for fresh parsley.

Peppered Steak with Dijon Sauce

Sweetheart Chocolate Mousse (page 166)

Luscious Chocolate Covered Strawberries (page 173)

no-bake desserts

Keep your kitchen cool with tasty sweet treats that don't require an oven.

Creamy Banana Pudding (page 178)

Easy Chocolate Cream-Filled Torte

Prep Time: 20 minutes
Chill Time: 30 minutes

> 1 frozen pound cake (10¾ ounces), thawed
> ½ cup powdered sugar
> ¼ cup HERSHEY'S Cocoa
> 1 cup (½ pint) cold whipping cream
> 1 teaspoon vanilla extract
>   Chocolate Glaze (recipe follows)
>   Sliced almonds (optional)

1. Cut cake horizontally to make 4 layers. Stir together sugar and cocoa in medium bowl. Add whipping cream and vanilla; beat until stiff.

2. Place bottom cake layer on serving platter. Spread ⅓ of the whipped cream mixture on cake layer. Place next cake layer on top of mixture; continue layering whipped cream mixture and cake until all have been used.

3. Prepare Chocolate Glaze; spoon over top of cake, allowing to drizzle down sides. Garnish with almonds, if desired. Refrigerate until ready to serve. Cover; refrigerate leftover torte. *Makes 8 to 10 servings*

Chocolate Glaze

> 2 tablespoons butter or margarine
> 2 tablespoons HERSHEY'S Cocoa
> 2 tablespoons water
> 1 cup powdered sugar
> ¼ to ½ teaspoon almond extract

Melt butter in small saucepan over low heat. Add cocoa and water. Cook, stirring constantly, until smooth and slightly thickened. Do not boil. Remove from heat. Gradually add powdered sugar and almond extract, beating with whisk until smooth. *Makes about ½ cup glaze*

Easy Chocolate Cream-Filled Torte

Toll House® Famous Fudge

1½ cups granulated sugar

⅔ cup (5 fluid-ounce can) NESTLÉ® CARNATION® Evaporated Milk

2 tablespoons butter or margarine

¼ teaspoon salt

2 cups miniature marshmallows

1½ cups (9 ounces) NESTLÉ® TOLL HOUSE® Semi-Sweet Chocolate Morsels

½ cup chopped pecans or walnuts (optional)

1 teaspoon vanilla extract

LINE 8-inch-square baking pan with foil.

COMBINE sugar, evaporated milk, butter and salt in medium, *heavy-duty* saucepan. Bring to a *full rolling boil* over medium heat, stirring constantly. Boil, stirring constantly, for 4 to 5 minutes. Remove from heat.

STIR in marshmallows, morsels, nuts and vanilla extract. Stir vigorously for 1 minute or until marshmallows are melted. Pour into prepared baking pan; refrigerate for 2 hours or until firm. Lift from pan; remove foil. Cut into pieces.   *Makes 49 pieces*

For Milk Chocolate Fudge: SUBSTITUTE 1¾ cups (11.5-ounce package) NESTLÉ® TOLL HOUSE® Milk Chocolate Morsels for Semi-Sweet Morsels.

For Butterscotch Fudge: SUBSTITUTE 1⅔ cups (11-ounce package) NESTLÉ® TOLL HOUSE® Butterscotch Flavored Morsels for Semi-Sweet Morsels.

For Peanutty Chocolate Fudge: SUBSTITUTE 1⅔ cups (11-ounce package) NESTLÉ® TOLL HOUSE® Peanut Butter & Milk Chocolate Morsels for Semi-Sweet Morsels and ½ cup chopped peanuts for pecans or walnuts.

Toll House® Famous Fudge

Ambrosia

1 can (20 ounces) DOLE® Pineapple Chunks
1 can (11 or 15 ounces) DOLE® Mandarin Oranges
1 firm, large DOLE® Banana, sliced (optional)
1½ cups DOLE® Seedless Grapes
1 cup miniature marshmallows
1 cup flaked coconut
½ cup pecan halves or coarsely chopped nuts
1 cup vanilla yogurt or sour cream
1 tablespoon brown sugar

Drain pineapple chunks and mandarin oranges. In large bowl, combine pineapple chunks, mandarin oranges, banana, grapes, marshmallows, coconut and nuts. In 1-quart measure, combine yogurt and brown sugar. Stir into fruit mixture. Refrigerate, covered, 1 hour or overnight.

Makes 4 servings

Milk Chocolate Almond Brickle

1¼ cups almonds, toasted and coarsely chopped
1 cup (2 sticks) butter
1½ cups packed brown sugar
1¾ cups (11.5-ounce package) NESTLÉ® TOLL HOUSE® Milk Chocolate Morsels

SPRINKLE nuts over bottom of well-greased 13×9-inch baking pan.

MELT butter in medium, *heavy-duty* saucepan over medium heat. Stir in sugar. Bring to a boil, stirring constantly, for 7 minutes. Pour hot mixture over nuts; let stand for 5 minutes. Sprinkle with morsels. Let stand for 5 minutes or until morsels are shiny and soft; spread evenly.

REFRIGERATE for about 20 minutes. Break into bite-size pieces.

Makes about 50 pieces

Ambrosia

Sweetheart Chocolate Mousse

   1 envelope unflavored gelatin
   2 tablespoons cold water
  ¼ cup boiling water
   1 cup sugar
  ½ cup HERSHEY'S Cocoa
   2 cups (1 pint) cold whipping cream
   2 teaspoons vanilla extract
    Fresh raspberries or sliced strawberries

1. Sprinkle gelatin over cold water in small bowl; let stand 2 minutes to soften. Add boiling water; stir until gelatin is completely dissolved and mixture is clear. Cool slightly.

2. Mix sugar and cocoa in large bowl; add whipping cream and vanilla. Beat on medium speed, scraping bottom of bowl occasionally, until mixture is stiff. Pour in gelatin mixture; beat until well blended.

3. Spoon into dessert dishes. Refrigerate at least 30 minutes before serving. Garnish with fruit. *Makes about 8 servings*

Cherries Jubilee

   2 (16-ounce) cans dark sweet cherries
  ¼ cup granulated sugar
   2 teaspoons cornstarch
   1 tablespoon grated orange peel
  ½ cup brandy or cognac, optional
   1 pound cake, cut into 16 slices, or 1-quart vanilla ice cream

Drain cherries, reserving syrup. Combine cherry syrup with sugar and cornstarch in a chafing dish or electric skillet. Cook, stirring constantly, over medium heat about 5 minutes, or until smooth and clear. Add cherries and orange peel; heat thoroughly.

Gently heat brandy or cognac in a small saucepan; pour over heated cherries. Flame, if desired. Stir gently and ladle over pound cake or ice cream.   *Makes 8 servings*

Favorite recipe from **Cherry Marketing Institute**

Strawberry Tiramisu

16 ounces BELGIOIOSO® Mascarpone Cheese
¾ cup powdered sugar
7 tablespoons marsala wine, divided
1 pint strawberries
¾ cup boiling water
2 tablespoons granulated sugar
2½ teaspoons instant espresso powder or instant coffee powder
1 (3½-ounce) package Champagne biscuits (ladyfinger-style cookies)
1 ounce bittersweet or semi-sweet chocolate, grated

Blend mascarpone, powdered sugar and 5 tablespoons marsala in food processor until smooth. Slice ½ pint strawberries; cut remaining ½ pint into halves.

Combine boiling water, granulated sugar and espresso powder in medium bowl; stir to dissolve. Stir in remaining 2 tablespoons marsala. Dip 1 biscuit briefly into espresso mixture, turning to coat. Place flat side up on bottom of 8-inch square glass baking dish with 2-inch-high sides. Repeat with enough biscuits to cover bottom of baking dish.

Spread ⅔ of BelGioioso mascarpone mixture over biscuits. Cover with sliced strawberries. Dip more biscuits into espresso mixture and arrange over sliced strawberries in dish, covering completely and trimming to fit. Spread remaining mascarpone mixture over biscuits. Sprinkle with grated chocolate. Arrange halved strawberries around edge of dish. Cover and refrigerate until set, at least 4 hours. Cut into squares and serve.   *Makes 4 to 6 servings*

Cinnamon & Raisin Rice Pudding with Caramelized Apples and Pecans

PREP TIME: 5 minutes
COOK TIME: 45 minutes

- 1 package UNCLE BEN'S® Cinnamon & Raisins Rice Pudding
- 1 large apple
- 1 teaspoon lemon juice
- ⅔ cup sugar
- 3 tablespoons butter
- ½ cup whole pecans
- 1 tablespoon apple cider vinegar

PREP: CLEAN: Wash hands. Core apple and slice in half, then slice each half into 4 to 6 slices. Place in bowl with lemon juice and enough water to cover. Set aside.

COOK: Prepare pudding according to package directions. Keep warm. In medium saucepan, cook sugar over medium heat until melted, golden and caramelized. Add butter and stir. Drain apples. Carefully add apples and pecans to caramelized sugar. Cook until apples are tender. Remove apples and pecans from pan. Add apple cider vinegar and cook 1 minute or until most of vinegar evaporates.

SERVE: Place individual servings of rice pudding in bowls. Top with apples and pecans. Drizzle generously with caramel sauce.

CHILL: Refrigerate leftovers immediately.

Makes 4 servings

Cinnamon & Raisin Rice Pudding with Caramelized Apples and Pecans

Strawberry Yogurt Tarts

Preparation Time: 15 minutes
Chilling Time: 1 hour

> 1 (8-ounce) carton strawberry yogurt
> 2 cups COOL WHIP® Whipped Topping, thawed, divided
> 1 (4-ounce) package READY CRUST® Mini-Graham Cracker Crusts
> 1 pint fresh strawberries, cut into halves

1. Blend yogurt and 1 cup whipped topping in small bowl.

2. Spoon yogurt mixture evenly into crusts. Arrange 2 strawberry halves around yogurt on each tart.

3. Garnish with remaining 1 cup whipped topping. Chill 1 hour or until firm.

Makes 6 tarts

White Chocolate Mousse

> 1 cup vanilla milk chips *or* 7 ounces white chocolate, chopped
> ¼ cup hot water
> 2 teaspoons WATKINS® Vanilla
> 2 cups heavy whipping cream
> ½ cup sifted powdered sugar

Melt vanilla chips in top of double boiler or in microwave. Add hot water and vanilla; mix until smooth. Cool completely. Beat cream until it begins to thicken. Add sugar; continue beating until soft peaks form. Stir large spoonful of whipped cream into vanilla chip mixture, then fold mixture back into remaining whipped cream. Spoon mousse into individual custard cups or 4-cup mold. Refrigerate until thoroughly chilled. Serve cold.   *Makes 8 servings*

Strawberry Yogurt Tarts

Double Chocolate Delight

   3 tablespoons butter or margarine, melted
   2 tablespoons sugar
   1 cup graham cracker crumbs
  ½ cup milk
   1 HERSHEY'S Milk Chocolate Bar (8 ounces), broken into pieces
  ½ cup HERSHEY'S MINI CHIPS™ Semi-Sweet Chocolate Chips
   1 cup (½ pint) cold whipping cream
     Sweetened whipped cream
     Sliced sweetened strawberries

1. Stir together butter and sugar in small bowl. Add graham cracker crumbs; mix well. Press mixture firmly onto bottom of 8-inch square pan. Refrigerate 1 to 2 hours or until firm.

2. Meanwhile, heat milk in small saucepan just until it begins to boil; remove from heat. Immediately add chocolate bar pieces and small chocolate chips; stir until chocolate melts and mixture is smooth. Pour into medium bowl; cool to room temperature.

3. Beat whipping cream in small bowl on high speed of mixer until stiff; fold gently into chocolate mixture. Pour into prepared crust; freeze several hours or until firm. Cut into squares. Just before serving, garnish with sweetened whipped cream and strawberries.

Makes 6 to 8 servings

Peanut Buster Bar Dessert

2½ cups crushed round chocolate sandwich cookies
6 tablespoons butter, softened
2 quarts vanilla ice cream or ice milk, slightly softened
2 cups powdered sugar
1½ cups evaporated milk
⅔ cup semi-sweet chocolate chips
½ cup (1 stick) butter
1½ teaspoons WATKINS® Vanilla
1½ cups Spanish peanuts

Mix cookie crumbs and 6 tablespoons softened butter in medium bowl; pat into 13×9-inch baking dish. Chill in freezer until set. Pack ice cream into chocolate crust; return to freezer.

Combine powdered sugar, milk, chocolate chips and ½ cup butter in medium saucepan; bring to a boil over medium heat, stirring constantly, until melted and smooth. Remove from heat and add vanilla; let sauce cool slightly. Sprinkle peanuts over ice cream; top with chocolate sauce. Return to freezer until frozen. *Makes 18 servings*

Luscious Chocolate Covered Strawberries

3 squares (1 ounce each) semi-sweet chocolate
2 tablespoons I CAN'T BELIEVE IT'S NOT BUTTER!® Spread
1 tablespoon coffee liqueur (optional)
6 to 8 large strawberries with stems

In small microwave-safe bowl, microwave chocolate and I Can't Believe It's Not Butter!® Spread at HIGH (Full Power) 1 minute or until chocolate is melted; stir until smooth. Stir in liqueur. Dip strawberries in chocolate mixture, then refrigerate on waxed paper-lined baking sheet until chocolate is set, at least 1 hour. *Makes 6 to 8 strawberries*

Englishman's Trifles

Prep Time: 20 minutes

> 1 box (10 ounces) BIRDS EYE® frozen Strawberries*
> 1 package (3.4 ounces) vanilla instant pudding
> 1½ cups milk
> 1 cup thawed frozen whipped topping
> 8 thin slices fresh or thawed frozen pound cake
> ½ cup toasted sliced almonds
> ¼ cup mini semisweet chocolate chips (optional)

Or, substitute Birds Eye® frozen Raspberries.

• Thaw strawberries according to package directions.

• Prepare pudding with 1½ cups milk according to package directions. Let stand 5 minutes; gently stir in whipped topping.

• Place 1 slice cake in each of 4 individual serving bowls. Spoon half the strawberries over cake. Top with half the pudding mixture, almonds and chocolate chips.

• Repeat layers of cake, strawberries, pudding, almonds and chips. Cover and chill until ready to serve.   *Makes 4 servings*

Englishman's Trifles

Cherry-Berry Crumble

Prep Time: 10 minutes

1 (21-ounce) can cherry pie filling

2 cups fresh or frozen raspberries

1 (14-ounce) can EAGLE BRAND® Sweetened Condensed Milk
   (NOT evaporated milk)

1½ cups granola

1. In medium saucepan over medium heat, cook and stir cherry pie filling and raspberries until heated through. Stir in EAGLE BRAND®; cook and stir 1 minute.

2. Spoon into 6 individual dessert dishes. Sprinkle with granola; garnish as desired. Serve warm. Store leftovers covered in refrigerator.   *Makes 6 servings*

Peach-Berry Crumble: Substitute peach pie filling for cherry pie filling.

Cherry-Rhubarb Crumble: Substitute fresh or frozen sliced rhubarb for raspberries. In medium saucepan over medium-high heat, cook and stir pie filling and rhubarb until bubbly. Cook and stir 5 minutes more. Proceed as directed above.

Vanilla Ice Cream

1 can (14 ounces) sweetened condensed milk

½ cup egg substitute

2 tablespoons water

4 teaspoons WATKINS® Vanilla*

2 cups heavy whipping cream, whipped

Substitute other Watkins extracts for Vanilla, if desired. Amounts may have to be adjusted for each.

Combine condensed milk, egg substitute, water and vanilla in medium bowl; mix well. Fold mixture into whipped cream. Transfer to plastic container, cover and freeze for at least 6 hours or overnight.   *Makes about 6 cups*

Cherry-Berry Crumble

Creamy Banana Pudding

Prep Time: 15 minutes

> 1 (14-ounce) can EAGLE BRAND® Sweetened Condensed
>   Milk (NOT evaporated milk)
> 1½ cups cold water
> 1 (4-serving-size) package instant vanilla pudding and pie
>   filling mix
> 2 cups (1 pint) whipping cream, whipped
> 36 vanilla wafers
> 3 medium bananas, sliced and dipped in lemon juice

1. In large bowl, combine EAGLE BRAND® and water. Add pudding mix; beat until well blended. Chill 5 minutes.

2. Fold in whipped cream. Spoon 1 cup pudding mixture into 2½-quart glass serving bowl or divide it among 8 to 10 individual serving dishes.

3. Top with one-third each of vanilla wafers, bananas and pudding mixture. Repeat layering twice, ending with pudding mixture. Chill. Garnish as desired. Store leftovers covered in refrigerator.   *Makes 8 to 10 servings*

Traditional Rice Pudding

> 1 bag SUCCESS® Rice
> ⅓ cup sugar
> 1½ tablespoons cornstarch
> 2 eggs, slightly beaten
> 2 cups skim milk
> 2 tablespoons margarine
> 1 teaspoon vanilla
> ½ teaspoon cinnamon

Prepare rice according to package directions. Cool.

Combine sugar and cornstarch in medium saucepan. Add eggs and milk; mix well. Stir in rice. Bring to a boil over medium-high heat, stirring constantly. Remove from heat. Add margarine and vanilla; stir until margarine is melted. Pour into serving bowl; sprinkle with cinnamon. Garnish, if desired. *Makes 6 servings*

Vanilla Mousse in Fluted Chocolate Cups

¾ cup (7.25 ounce bottle) SMUCKER'S® Magic Shell Chocolate or Chocolate Fudge Ice Cream Topping

1 package (24) foil baking cups (1¾ inch in diameter)

⅔ cup evaporated milk, thoroughly chilled

1 egg

¼ cup sugar

Salt

1 teaspoon vanilla

24 fresh mint leaves, if desired

24 maraschino cherry slices (optional)

Pour Magic Shell into small bowl. With small, dry pastry brush, thinly and evenly coat insides of baking cups with Magic Shell. Chill in freezer for several minutes. Coat and freeze each cup at least 3 more times. Store cups in freezer.

Whip evaporated milk until stiff. Beat in egg, sugar, a pinch of salt and vanilla. Spoon or pipe mousse into fluted chocolate cups. Freeze until firm. Before serving, carefully remove foil and garnish each cup with 1 mint leaf and 1 maraschino cherry slice. For extended storage, cover tops of cups lightly with plastic wrap and store in freezer up to 1 week.

Makes 24 servings

Chocolate Mint Truffles

1¾ cups (11.5-ounce package) NESTLÉ® TOLL HOUSE® Milk Chocolate Morsels

1 cup (6 ounces) NESTLÉ® TOLL HOUSE® Semi-Sweet Chocolate Morsels

¾ cup heavy whipping cream

1 tablespoon peppermint extract

1½ cups finely chopped walnuts, toasted, or NESTLÉ® TOLL HOUSE® Baking Cocoa

LINE baking sheet with wax paper.

PLACE milk chocolate and semi-sweet morsels in large mixer bowl. Heat cream to a gentle boil in small saucepan; pour over morsels. Let stand for 1 minute; stir until smooth. Stir in peppermint extract. Cover with plastic wrap; refrigerate for 35 to 45 minutes or until slightly thickened. Stir just until color lightens slightly. (*Do not* overmix or truffles will be grainy.)

DROP by rounded teaspoon onto prepared baking sheet; refrigerate for 10 to 15 minutes. Shape into balls; roll in walnuts or cocoa. Store in airtight container in refrigerator.

Makes about 48 truffles

Variation: After rolling chocolate mixture into balls, freeze for 30 to 40 minutes. Microwave 1¾ cups (11.5-ounce package) NESTLÉ® TOLL HOUSE® Milk Chocolate Morsels and 3 tablespoons vegetable shortening in medium, uncovered, microwave-safe bowl on MEDIUM-HIGH (70%) power for 1 minute. STIR. Morsels may retain some of their original shape. If necessary, microwave at additional 10- to 15-second intervals, stirring just until morsels are melted. Dip truffles into chocolate mixture; shake off excess. Place on foil-lined baking sheets. Refrigerate for 15 to 20 minutes or until set. Store in airtight container in refrigerator.

Chocolate Mint Truffles

Original Nestlé® Toll House® Chocolate Chip Cookies (page 197)

Cookie Pizza (page 196)

Nothing beats the tempting aroma of cookies baking — except tasting them fresh out of the oven!

cookies by the dozen

Jumbo 3-Chip Cookies (page 209)

Pumpkin Harvest Bars

1¾ cups all-purpose flour

2 teaspoons baking powder

1 teaspoon grated orange peel

1 teaspoon ground cinnamon

½ teaspoon salt

½ teaspoon ground nutmeg

¼ teaspoon ground ginger

¼ teaspoon ground cloves

¾ cup sugar

½ cup MOTT'S® Natural Apple Sauce

½ cup solid-pack pumpkin

1 whole egg

1 egg white

2 tablespoons vegetable oil

½ cup raisins

1. Preheat oven to 350°F. Spray 13×9-inch baking pan with nonstick cooking spray.

2. In small bowl, combine flour, baking powder, orange peel, cinnamon, salt, nutmeg, ginger and cloves.

3. In large bowl, combine sugar, apple sauce, pumpkin, whole egg, egg white and oil.

4. Add flour mixture to apple sauce mixture; stir until well blended. Stir in raisins. Spread batter into prepared pan.

5. Bake 25 to 30 minutes or until toothpick inserted in center comes out clean. Cool on wire rack 15 minutes; cut into 16 bars. *Makes 16 servings*

Pumpkin Harvest Bars

Coconut Clouds

2⅔ cups flaked coconut, divided
1 package DUNCAN HINES® Moist Deluxe® Classic Yellow Cake Mix
1 egg
½ cup vegetable oil
¼ cup water
1 teaspoon almond extract

1. Preheat oven to 350°F. Reserve 1⅓ cups coconut in medium bowl.

2. Combine cake mix, egg, oil, water and almond extract in large bowl. Beat at low speed with electric mixer. Stir in remaining 1⅓ cups coconut. Drop rounded teaspoonful of dough into reserved coconut. Roll to cover lightly. Place on ungreased baking sheet. Repeat with remaining dough, placing balls 2 inches apart. Bake at 350°F for 10 to 12 minutes or until light golden brown. Cool 1 minute on baking sheets. Remove to cooling racks. Cool completely. Store in airtight container.   *Makes 3½ dozen cookies*

tip:

To save time when forming dough into balls, use a 1-inch spring-operated cookie scoop. Spring-operated cookie scoops are available at kitchen specialty shops.

Coconut Clouds

Choc-Oat-Chip Cookies

1 cup (2 sticks) butter or margarine, softened

1 cup firmly packed brown sugar

½ cup granulated sugar

2 eggs

2 tablespoons milk

2 teaspoons vanilla

1¾ cups all-purpose flour

1 teaspoon baking soda

½ teaspoon salt (optional)

2½ cups QUAKER® Oats (quick or old fashioned, uncooked)

2 cups semisweet chocolate pieces

1 cup coarsely chopped nuts (optional)

Preheat oven to 375°F. Beat together butter and sugars until creamy. Add eggs, milk and vanilla; beat well. Add flour, baking soda and salt; mix well. Stir in oats, chocolate pieces and nuts; mix well. Drop by rounded tablespoonfuls onto ungreased cookie sheets.* Bake at 375°F for 9 to 10 minutes for a chewy cookie or 12 to 13 minutes for a crisp cookie. Cool 1 minute on cookie sheets; remove to wire racks. Cool completely. Store in tightly covered container.

Makes about 5 dozen cookies

For bar cookies: Press dough evenly into ungreased 13×9-inch metal baking pan. Bake 30 to 35 minutes or until light golden brown. Cool completely; cut into bars. Store tightly covered.

High altitude adjustment: Increase flour to 2 cups.

Variations: Prepare cookies as recipe directs, except substitute 1 cup of any of the following for 1 cup chocolate pieces: raisins, chopped dried apricots, dried cherries, crushed toffee pieces, candy-coated chocolate pieces or white chocolate baking pieces.

Choc-Oat-Chip Cookies

Mini Chip Snowball Cookies

1½ cups (3 sticks) butter or margarine, softened
¾ cup powdered sugar
1 tablespoon vanilla extract
½ teaspoon salt
3 cups all-purpose flour
2 cups (12-ounce package) NESTLÉ® TOLL HOUSE® Semi-Sweet Chocolate Mini Morsels
½ cup finely chopped nuts
Powdered sugar

PREHEAT oven to 375°F.

BEAT butter, sugar, vanilla extract and salt in large mixer bowl until creamy. Gradually beat in flour; stir in morsels and nuts. Shape level tablespoons of dough into 1¼-inch balls. Place on ungreased baking sheets.

BAKE for 10 to 12 minutes or until cookies are set and lightly browned. Remove from oven. Sift powdered sugar over hot cookies on baking sheets. Cool on baking sheets for 10 minutes; remove to wire racks to cool completely. Sprinkle with additional powdered sugar, if desired. Store in airtight containers.

Makes about 5 dozen cookies

Mini Chip Snowball Cookies

Chocolate Peanut Butter Cup Cookies

1 cup semisweet chocolate chips

2 squares (1 ounce each) unsweetened baking chocolate

1 cup sugar

½ CRISCO® Butter Flavor Stick or ½ cup CRISCO® Butter Flavor Shortening

2 eggs

1 teaspoon salt

1 teaspoon vanilla

1½ cups plus 2 tablespoons PILLSBURY BEST® All-Purpose Flour

½ teaspoon baking soda

¾ cup finely chopped peanuts

36 miniature peanut butter cups, unwrapped

1 cup peanut butter chips

1. Heat oven to 350°F. Place sheets of foil on countertop for cooling cookies.

2. Combine chocolate chips and chocolate squares in microwave-safe measuring cup or bowl. Microwave at 50% power (MEDIUM). Stir after 2 minutes. Repeat until smooth (or melt on rangetop in small saucepan over very low heat). Cool slightly.

3. Combine sugar and ½ cup CRISCO Shortening in large bowl. Beat at medium speed of electric mixer until blended and crumbly. Beat in eggs, one at a time, then salt and vanilla. Reduce speed to low. Add chocolate slowly. Mix until well blended. Stir in flour and baking soda with spoon until well blended. Shape dough into 1¼-inch balls. Roll in nuts. Place 2 inches apart on ungreased baking sheet.

4. Bake at 350°F for 8 to 10 minutes or until set. *Do not overbake.* Press peanut butter cup into center of each cookie immediately. Cool 2 minutes on baking sheet. Remove cookies to foil to cool completely.

5. Place peanut butter chips in heavy resealable sandwich bag. Seal. Microwave at 50% power (MEDIUM). Knead bag after 1 minute. Repeat until smooth (or melt by placing bag in hot water). Cut tiny tip off corner of bag. Squeeze out and drizzle over cookies.

Makes 3 dozen cookies

Chocolate Chip Cookie Bars

1¼ cups firmly packed light brown sugar
¾ CRISCO® Butter Flavor Stick or ¾ cup CRISCO® Butter Flavor Shortening plus
    additional for greasing
2 tablespoons milk
1 tablespoon vanilla
2 eggs
1¾ cups PILLSBURY BEST® All-Purpose Flour
1 teaspoon salt
¾ teaspoon baking soda
1 cup (6 ounces) semisweet chocolate chips
1 cup coarsely chopped pecans* (optional)

If pecans are omitted, add an additional ½ cup semisweet chocolate chips.

1. Heat oven to 350°F. Grease 13×9-inch baking pan. Place wire rack on countertop for cooling bars.

2. Combine brown sugar, ¾ cup CRISCO Shortening, milk and vanilla in large bowl. Beat at medium speed of electric mixer until well blended. Add eggs; beat well.

3. Combine flour, salt and baking soda. Add to CRISCO Shortening mixture; beat at low speed just until blended. Stir in chocolate chips and nuts, if desired.

4. Press dough evenly onto bottom of prepared pan.

5. Bake at 350°F for 20 to 25 minutes or until lightly browned and firm in the center. *Do not overbake.* Cool completely on cooling rack. Cut into 2×1½-inch bars.

Makes about 3 dozen bars

Peanutty Cranberry Bars

½ cup (1 stick) butter or margarine, softened
½ cup granulated sugar
¼ cup packed light brown sugar
1 cup all-purpose flour
1 cup quick-cooking rolled oats
¼ teaspoon baking soda
¼ teaspoon salt
1 cup REESE'S® Peanut Butter Chips
1½ cups fresh or frozen whole cranberries
⅔ cup light corn syrup
½ cup water
1 teaspoon vanilla extract

1. Heat oven to 350°F. Grease 8-inch square baking pan.

2. Beat butter, granulated sugar and brown sugar in medium bowl until fluffy. Stir together flour, oats, baking soda and salt; gradually add to butter mixture, mixing until mixture is consistency of coarse crumbs. Stir in peanut butter chips.

3. Reserve 1½ cups mixture for crumb topping. Firmly press remaining mixture evenly into prepared pan. Bake 15 minutes or until set.

4. Meanwhile, in medium saucepan, combine cranberries, corn syrup and water. Cook over medium heat, stirring occasionally, until mixture boils. Reduce heat; simmer 15 minutes, stirring occasionally. Remove from heat. Stir in vanilla. Spread evenly over baked layer. Sprinkle reserved 1½ cups crumb topping evenly over top.

5. Return to oven. Bake 15 to 20 minutes or until set. Cool completely in pan on wire rack. Cut into bars. *Makes about 16 bars*

Peanutty Cranberry Bars

Cookie Pizza

Prep Time: 15 minutes
Bake Time: 14 minutes

> 1 (18-ounce) package refrigerated sugar cookie dough
> 2 cups (12 ounces) semisweet chocolate chips
> 1 (14-ounce) can EAGLE BRAND® Sweetened Condensed Milk
>   (NOT evaporated milk)
> 2 cups candy-coated milk chocolate pieces
> 2 cups miniature marshmallows
> ½ cup peanuts

1. Preheat oven to 375°F. Divide cookie dough in half; press each half onto ungreased 12-inch pizza pan. Bake 10 minutes or until golden. Remove from oven.

2. In medium saucepan, melt chocolate chips with EAGLE BRAND®. Spread over crusts. Sprinkle with chocolate pieces, marshmallows and peanuts.

3. Bake 4 minutes or until marshmallows are lightly toasted. Cool. Cut into wedges.

Makes 2 pizzas (24 servings)

tip:

BE CREATIVE! Mix and match your favorite candy-coated milk chocolate pieces. To create a fun springtime treat, use pastel mini marshmallows and pastel candy-coated milk chocolate pieces.

Original Nestlé® Toll House® Chocolate Chip Cookies

2¼ cups all-purpose flour

  1 teaspoon baking soda

  1 teaspoon salt

  1 cup (2 sticks) butter or margarine, softened

¾ cup granulated sugar

¾ cup packed brown sugar

  1 teaspoon vanilla extract

  2 eggs

  2 cups (12-ounce package) NESTLÉ® TOLL HOUSE® Semi-Sweet Chocolate Morsels

  1 cup chopped nuts

PREHEAT oven to 375°F.

COMBINE flour, baking soda and salt in small bowl. Beat butter, granulated sugar, brown sugar and vanilla extract in large mixer bowl until creamy. Add eggs, one at a time, beating well after each addition. Gradually beat in flour mixture. Stir in morsels and nuts. Drop by rounded tablespoonfuls onto ungreased baking sheets.

BAKE for 9 to 11 minutes or until golden brown. Cool on baking sheets for 2 minutes; remove to wire racks to cool completely. *Makes about 5 dozen cookies*

Pan Cookie Variation: GREASE 15×10-inch jelly-roll pan. Prepare dough as above. Spread in prepared pan. Bake for 20 to 25 minutes or until golden brown. Cool in pan on wire rack. Makes 4 dozen bars.

Lemon Bars

1 package DUNCAN HINES® Moist Deluxe® Lemon Supreme Cake Mix

3 eggs, divided

⅓ cup butter-flavor shortening

½ cup granulated sugar

¼ cup lemon juice

2 teaspoons grated lemon peel

½ teaspoon baking powder

¼ teaspoon salt

Confectioners' sugar

1. Preheat oven to 350°F.

2. Combine cake mix, 1 egg and shortening in large mixing bowl. Beat at low speed with electric mixer until crumbs form. Reserve 1 cup. Pat remaining mixture lightly into *ungreased* 13×9-inch pan. Bake at 350°F for 15 minutes or until lightly browned.

3. Combine remaining 2 eggs, granulated sugar, lemon juice, lemon peel, baking powder and salt in medium mixing bowl. Beat at medium speed with electric mixer until light and foamy. Pour over hot crust. Sprinkle with reserved crumb mixture.

4. Bake at 350°F for 15 minutes or until lightly browned. Sprinkle with confectioners' sugar. Cool in pan. Cut into bars.   *Makes 30 to 32 bars*

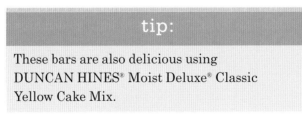

tip:

These bars are also delicious using DUNCAN HINES® Moist Deluxe® Classic Yellow Cake Mix.

Lemon Bars

Chocolate Pistachio Cookies

  2 cups shelled pistachio or macadamia nuts, finely chopped, divided
1¾ cups all-purpose flour
  ¼ cup unsweetened cocoa powder
  ¾ teaspoon baking soda
  ½ teaspoon salt
  ¾ cup plus 1 tablespoon I CAN'T BELIEVE IT'S NOT BUTTER!® Spread, divided
  1 cup granulated sugar
  ¾ cup firmly packed brown sugar
  2 eggs
  3 squares (1 ounce each) unsweetened chocolate, melted
  ½ teaspoon vanilla extract
  ⅛ teaspoon almond extract
1½ squares (1 ounce each) unsweetened chocolate
  2 tablespoons confectioners' sugar

Preheat oven to 375°F. Lightly spray baking sheets with I Can't Believe It's Not Butter!® Spray; set aside. Reserve 3 tablespoons pistachios for garnish.

In medium bowl, combine flour, cocoa powder, baking soda and salt; set aside.

In large bowl, with electric mixer, beat ¾ cup I Can't Believe It's Not Butter!® Spread, granulated sugar and brown sugar until light and fluffy, about 5 minutes. Beat in eggs, one at a time, beating 30 seconds after each addition. Beat in melted chocolate and extracts. Beat in flour mixture just until blended. Stir in pistachios.

On prepared baking sheets, drop dough by rounded tablespoonfuls, 1 inch apart. Bake one sheet at a time 8 minutes or until tops are puffed and dry but still soft when touched. *Do not overbake.* On wire rack, cool 5 minutes; remove from sheets and cool completely.

For icing, in microwave-safe bowl, melt 1½ squares chocolate with remaining 1 tablespoon I Can't Believe It's Not Butter! Spread at HIGH (Full Power) 1 minute or until chocolate is melted; stir until smooth. Stir in confectioners' sugar. Lightly spread ¼ teaspoon icing on each cookie, then sprinkle with reserved pistachios. Let stand 20 minutes before serving.

Makes about 3½ dozen cookies

Chocolate Pistachio Cookies

Peanut Butter and Chocolate Cookie Sandwich Cookies

½ cup REESE'S® Peanut Butter Chips

3 tablespoons plus ½ cup (1 stick) butter or margarine, softened and divided

1¼ cups sugar, divided

¼ cup light corn syrup

1 egg

1 teaspoon vanilla extract

2 cups plus 2 tablespoons all-purpose flour, divided

2 teaspoons baking soda

¼ teaspoon salt

½ cup HERSHEY'S Cocoa

5 tablespoons butter or margarine, melted

Additional sugar

About 2 dozen large marshmallows

1. Heat oven to 350°F. Melt peanut butter chips and 3 tablespoons softened butter in small saucepan over very low heat. Remove from heat; cool slightly.

2. Beat remaining ½ cup softened butter and 1 cup sugar in large bowl until fluffy. Add corn syrup, egg and vanilla; blend thoroughly. Stir together 2 cups flour, baking soda and salt; add to butter mixture, blending well. Remove 1¼ cups batter and place in small bowl; with wooden spoon, stir in remaining 2 tablespoons flour and melted peanut butter chip mixture.

3. Blend cocoa, remaining ¼ cup sugar and 5 tablespoons melted butter into remaining batter. Refrigerate both doughs 5 to 10 minutes or until firm enough to handle. Shape each dough into 1-inch balls; roll in sugar. Place on ungreased cookie sheets.

4. Bake 10 to 11 minutes or until set. Cool slightly; remove from cookie sheets to wire racks. Cool completely. Place 1 marshmallow on flat side of 1 chocolate cookie. Microwave at MEDIUM (50% power) 10 seconds or until marshmallow is softened. Place a peanut butter cookie over marshmallow; press down lightly. Repeat for remaining cookies. Serve immediately.   *Makes about 2 dozen sandwich cookies*

Peanut Butter and Chocolate Cookie Sandwich Cookies

Gingersnaps

2½ cups all-purpose flour

1½ teaspoons ground ginger

1 teaspoon baking soda

1 teaspoon ground allspice

½ teaspoon salt

1½ cups sugar

2 tablespoons margarine, softened

½ cup MOTT'S® Apple Sauce

¼ cup GRANDMA'S® Molasses

1. Preheat oven to 375°F. Spray cookie sheets with nonstick cooking spray.

2. In medium bowl, sift together flour, ginger, baking soda, allspice and salt.

3. In large bowl, beat sugar and margarine with electric mixer at medium speed until blended. Whisk in apple sauce and molasses.

4. Add flour mixture to apple sauce mixture; stir until well blended.

5. Drop rounded tablespoonfuls of dough 1 inch apart onto prepared cookie sheets. Flatten each slightly with moistened fingertips.

6. Bake 12 to 15 minutes or until firm. Cool completely on wire rack.

Makes 3 dozen cookies

Gingersnaps

Snow-Covered Almond Crescents

1 cup (2 sticks) margarine or butter, softened

¾ cup powdered sugar

½ teaspoon almond extract or 2 teaspoons vanilla extract

2 cups all-purpose flour

¼ teaspoon salt (optional)

1 cup QUAKER® Oats (quick or old fashioned, uncooked)

½ cup finely chopped almonds

Additional powdered sugar

Preheat oven to 325°F. Beat margarine, ¾ cup powdered sugar and almond extract until fluffy. Add flour and salt; mix until well blended. Stir in oats and almonds. Shape level measuring tablespoonfuls of dough into crescents. Place on ungreased cookie sheets about 2 inches apart.

Bake 14 to 17 minutes or until bottoms are light golden brown. Remove to wire racks. Sift additional powdered sugar generously over warm cookies. Cool completely. Store tightly covered.

Makes about 4 dozen cookies

Snow-Covered Almond Crescents

Chocolate Nut Bars

Prep Time: 10 minutes
Bake Time: 33 to 38 minutes

> 1¾ cups graham cracker crumbs
> ½ cup (1 stick) butter or margarine, melted
> 2 cups (12 ounces) semisweet chocolate chips, divided
> 1 (14-ounce) can EAGLE BRAND® Sweetened Condensed Milk
>   (NOT evaporated milk)
> 1 teaspoon vanilla extract
> 1 cup chopped nuts

1. Preheat oven to 375°F. In medium bowl, combine graham cracker crumbs and butter; press firmly on bottom of ungreased 13×9-inch baking pan. Bake 8 minutes. Reduce oven temperature to 350°F.

2. In small saucepan over low heat, melt 1 cup chocolate chips with EAGLE BRAND® and vanilla. Spread chocolate mixture over baked crust. Top with remaining 1 cup chocolate chips and nuts; press down firmly.

3. Bake 25 to 30 minutes. Cool. Chill, if desired. Cut into bars. Store loosely covered at room temperature.   *Makes 2 to 3 dozen bars*

Thumbprint Cookies

> 1 cup (2 sticks) butter or margarine
> ¼ cup sugar
> 1 teaspoon almond extract
> 2 cups all-purpose flour
> ½ teaspoon salt
> 1 cup finely chopped nuts (optional)
>   SMUCKER'S® Preserves or Jams (any flavor)

1. Preheat oven to 400°F. Combine butter and sugar; beat until light and fluffy. Blend in almond extract. Add flour and salt; mix well.

2. Shape level tablespoonfuls of dough into balls; roll in nuts, if desired. Place on ungreased baking sheets; flatten slightly. Indent centers; fill with preserves or jams.

3. Bake at 400°F for 10 to 12 minutes or just until lightly browned.

Makes 2½ dozen cookies

Jumbo 3-Chip Cookies

4 cups all-purpose flour
1 teaspoon baking powder
1 teaspoon baking soda
1½ cups (3 sticks) butter, softened
1¼ cups granulated sugar
1¼ cups packed brown sugar
2 eggs
1 tablespoon vanilla extract
1 cup (6 ounces) NESTLÉ® TOLL HOUSE® Milk Chocolate Morsels
1 cup (6 ounces) NESTLÉ® TOLL HOUSE® Semi-Sweet Chocolate Morsels
½ cup NESTLÉ® TOLL HOUSE® Premier White Morsels
1 cup chopped nuts

PREHEAT oven to 375°F.

COMBINE flour, baking powder and baking soda in medium bowl. Beat butter, granulated sugar and brown sugar in large mixer bowl until creamy. Beat in eggs and vanilla extract. Gradually beat in flour mixture. Stir in morsels and nuts. Drop dough by level ¼-cup measure 2 inches apart onto ungreased baking sheets.

BAKE for 12 to 14 minutes or until light golden brown. Cool on baking sheets for 2 minutes; remove to wire racks to cool completely.

Makes about 2 dozen cookies

Pumpkin Polka Dot Cookies

1¼ cups EQUAL® SPOONFUL*

½ cup (1 stick) butter or margarine, softened

3 tablespoons light molasses

1 cup canned pumpkin

1 egg

1½ teaspoons vanilla

1⅔ cups all-purpose flour

1 teaspoon baking powder

1¼ teaspoons ground cinnamon

½ teaspoon ground nutmeg

½ teaspoon ground ginger

½ teaspoon baking soda

¼ teaspoon salt

1 cup mini semi-sweet chocolate chips

May substitute 30 packets EQUAL® sweetener.

• Beat Equal®, butter and molasses until well combined. Mix in pumpkin, egg and vanilla until blended. Gradually stir in flour, baking powder, spices, baking soda and salt until well blended. Stir in chocolate chips.

• Drop by teaspoonfuls onto baking sheets sprayed with nonstick cooking spray. Bake in preheated 350°F oven 11 to 13 minutes. Remove from baking sheets and cool completely on wire rack. Store at room temperature in airtight container up to 1 week.

Makes about 4 dozen cookies

Pumpkin Polka Dot Cookies

Peanut Blossoms

48 HERSHEY'S KISSES® Brand Milk Chocolates

¾ cup REESE'S® Creamy or Crunchy Peanut Butter

½ cup shortening

⅓ cup granulated sugar

⅓ cup packed light brown sugar

1 egg

2 tablespoons milk

1 teaspoon vanilla extract

1½ cups all-purpose flour

1 teaspoon baking soda

½ teaspoon salt

Granulated sugar

1. Heat oven to 375°F. Remove wrappers from chocolates.

2. Beat peanut butter and shortening with electric mixer on medium speed in large bowl until well blended. Add ⅓ cup granulated sugar and brown sugar; beat until fluffy. Add egg, milk and vanilla; beat well. Stir together flour, baking soda and salt; gradually beat into peanut butter mixture.

3. Shape dough into 1-inch balls. Roll in additional granulated sugar; place on ungreased cookie sheet.

4. Bake 8 to 10 minutes or until lightly browned. Immediately press a chocolate into center of each cookie; cookies will crack around edges. Remove to wire racks and cool completely.

Makes about 4 dozen cookies

Peanut Blossoms

Colorful Cookie Buttons

1½ cups (3 sticks) butter, softened
½ cup granulated sugar
½ cup firmly packed light brown sugar
2 egg yolks
1 teaspoon vanilla extract
3½ cups all-purpose flour
1½ teaspoons baking powder
½ teaspoon salt
1 cup "M&M's"® Chocolate Mini Baking Bits

Preheat oven to 350°F. In large bowl cream butter and sugars until light and fluffy; beat in egg yolks and vanilla. In medium bowl combine flour, baking powder and salt; add to creamed mixture. Shape dough into 72 balls. For each cookie, place one ball on ungreased cookie sheet and flatten. Place 8 to 10 "M&M's"® Chocolate Mini Baking Bits on dough. Flatten second ball and place over "M&M's"® Chocolate Mini Baking Bits, pressing top and bottom dough together. Decorate top with remaining "M&M's"® Chocolate Mini Baking Bits. Repeat with remaining dough balls and "M&M's"® Chocolate Mini Baking Bits, placing cookies about 2 inches apart on cookie sheets. Bake 17 to 18 minutes. Cool 2 minutes on cookie sheets; cool completely on wire racks. Store in tightly covered container.

Makes 3 dozen cookies

Colorful Cookie Buttons

Hot Fudge Sundae Cake (page 245)

German Chocolate Cake (page 226)

cakes & pies

Slices of incredibly moist cakes and classic pies are perfect for every occasion.

Hershey's Red Velvet Cake (page 235)

Very Cherry Pie

4 cups frozen unsweetened tart cherries
1 cup dried tart cherries
1 cup granulated sugar
2 tablespoons quick-cooking tapioca
½ teaspoon almond extract
   Pastry for double-crust 9-inch pie
¼ teaspoon ground nutmeg
1 tablespoon butter

Combine frozen cherries, dried cherries, sugar, tapioca and almond extract in large mixing bowl; mix well. (It is not necessary to thaw cherries before using.) Let cherry mixture stand 15 minutes.

Line 9-inch pie plate with pastry; fill with cherry mixture. Sprinkle with nutmeg. Dot with butter. Cover with top crust, cutting slits for steam to escape. Or, cut top crust into strips for lattice top.

Bake in preheated 375°F oven about 1 hour or until crust is golden brown and filling is bubbly. If necessary, cover edge of crust with foil to prevent overbrowning.

Makes 8 servings

Note: Two (14.5-ounce) cans unsweetened tart cherries, well drained, can be substituted for frozen tart cherries. Dried cherries are available at gourmet and specialty food stores and at selected supermarkets.

Favorite recipe from **Cherry Marketing Institute**

Very Cherry Pie

Hershey's "Perfectly Chocolate" Chocolate Cake

  2 cups sugar

1¾ cups all-purpose flour

  ¾ cup HERSHEY'S Cocoa or HERSHEY'S Special Dark® Cocoa

1½ teaspoons baking powder

1½ teaspoons baking soda

  1 teaspoon salt

  2 eggs

  1 cup milk

  ½ cup vegetable oil

  2 teaspoons vanilla extract

  1 cup boiling water

      "Perfectly Chocolate" Chocolate Frosting (page 222)

1. Heat oven to 350°F. Grease and flour two 9-inch round baking pans.

2. Stir together sugar, flour, cocoa, baking powder, baking soda and salt in large bowl. Add eggs, milk, oil and vanilla; beat on medium speed of mixer 2 minutes. Stir in water. (Batter will be thin.) Pour batter evenly into prepared pans.

3. Bake 30 to 35 minutes or until wooden pick inserted into center comes out clean. Cool 10 minutes; remove from pans to wire racks. Cool completely.

4. Prepare "Perfectly Chocolate" Chocolate Frosting; spread between layers and over top and sides of cake.

Makes 8 to 10 servings

continued on page 222

Hershey's "Perfectly Chocolate"
Chocolate Cake

Hershey's "Perfectly Chocolate" Chocolate Cake, continued

"Perfectly Chocolate" Chocolate Frosting

½ cup (1 stick) butter or margarine
⅔ cup HERSHEY'S Cocoa
3 cups powdered sugar
⅓ cup milk
1 teaspoon vanilla extract

1. Melt butter. Stir in cocoa. Alternately add powdered sugar and milk, beating to spreading consistency.

2. Add small amount additional milk, if needed. Stir in vanilla.   *Makes about 2 cups*

Boston Cream Pie

1 package DUNCAN HINES® Moist Deluxe® Classic Yellow Cake Mix
2 containers (3½ ounces each) ready-to-eat vanilla pudding
1 container DUNCAN HINES® Chocolate Frosting

1. Preheat oven to 350°F. Grease and flour two 8- or 9-inch round pans.

2. Prepare, bake and cool cakes following package directions for basic recipe.

3. To assemble, place one cake layer on serving plate. Spread contents of 2 containers of vanilla pudding on top of cake. Top with second cake layer. Remove lid and foil top of Chocolate frosting container. Heat in microwave oven at HIGH (100% power) for 25 to 30 seconds. Stir. (Mixture should be thin.) Spread chocolate glaze over top of second cake layer. Refrigerate until ready to serve.   *Makes 12 to 16 servings*

Tip: For a richer flavor, substitute DUNCAN HINES® Butter Recipe Golden Cake Mix in place of Yellow Cake Mix.

Boston Cream Pie

Kahlúa® Black Forest Cake

1 package (18¼ ounces) chocolate fudge cake mix with pudding

3 eggs

¾ cup water

½ cup KAHLÚA® Liqueur

⅓ cup vegetable oil

1 can (16 ounces) vanilla or chocolate frosting

1 can (21 ounces) cherry pie filling

Chocolate sprinkles or chocolate shavings for garnish (optional)

Preheat oven to 350°F. Grease and flour 2 (9-inch) cake pans; set aside. In large mixer bowl, prepare cake mix using 3 eggs, ¾ cup water, Kahlúa® and ⅓ cup oil. Pour batter into prepared pans. Bake 25 to 35 minutes or until toothpick inserted in center comes out clean. Cool cakes in pans 10 minutes; turn layers out onto wire racks to cool completely.

Place one cake layer bottom side up on serving plate. Spread thick layer of frosting in circle, 1½ inches around outer edge of cake. Spoon half of cherry filling into center of cake layer to frosting edge. Top with second cake layer, bottom side down. Repeat with frosting and remaining cherry filling. Spread remaining frosting around side of cake. Decorate with chocolate sprinkles or shavings, if desired. *Makes 1 (9-inch) cake*

Kahlúa® Black Forest Cake

German Chocolate Cake

¼ cup HERSHEY'S Cocoa
½ cup boiling water
1 cup (2 sticks) plus 3 tablespoons butter or margarine, softened
2¼ cups sugar
1 teaspoon vanilla extract
4 eggs
2 cups all-purpose flour
1 teaspoon baking soda
½ teaspoon salt
1 cup buttermilk or sour milk*
Coconut Pecan Frosting (recipe follows)

*To sour milk: Use 1 tablespoon white vinegar plus milk to equal 1 cup.

1. Heat oven to 350°F. Grease and flour three 9-inch round baking pans. Combine cocoa and water in small bowl; stir until smooth. Set aside to cool.

2. Beat butter, sugar and vanilla in large bowl until fluffy. Add eggs, one at a time, beating well after each addition. Stir together flour, baking soda and salt; add alternately with chocolate mixture and buttermilk to butter mixture. Mix only until smooth. Pour batter into prepared pans.

3. Bake 25 to 30 minutes or until top springs back when touched lightly. Cool 5 minutes; remove from pans. Cool completely on wire rack. Prepare Coconut Pecan Frosting; spread between layers and over top. Garnish, if desired.   *Makes 10 to 12 servings*

Coconut Pecan Frosting

1 can (14 ounces) sweetened condensed milk (not evaporated milk)
3 egg yolks, slightly beaten
½ cup (1 stick) butter or margarine
1 teaspoon vanilla extract
1⅓ cups MOUNDS® Sweetened Coconut Flakes
1 cup chopped pecans

1. Place sweetened condensed milk, egg yolks and butter in medium saucepan. Cook over low heat, stirring constantly, until mixture is thickened and bubbly.

2. Remove from heat; stir in vanilla, coconut and pecans. Cool to room temperature.

Makes about 2⅔ cups

Delicious American Apple Pie

Preparation Time: 30 minutes
Bake Time: 45 minutes

> **Prepared frozen or refrigerated pastry for double-crust 9-inch pie**
> **¾ cup firmly packed DOMINO® Light Brown Sugar**
> **1 tablespoon all-purpose flour**
> **½ teaspoon cinnamon**
> **¼ teaspoon nutmeg**
> **⅛ teaspoon salt**
> **1 tablespoon grated lemon peel**
> **6 cups peeled, cored and thickly sliced apples**
> **1 tablespoon lemon juice**
> **2 tablespoons butter or margarine**

Heat oven to 425°F. Line 9-inch pie pan with one half of pastry. Combine sugar, flour, cinnamon, nutmeg, salt and lemon peel in large bowl. Add apples and toss to coat evenly. Spoon apple mixture into pastry-lined pie pan. Sprinkle with lemon juice and dot with butter. Top with remaining pastry. Trim and flute edges. Cut slits in top crust to allow steam to escape. Bake at 425°F for 40 to 45 minutes or until golden brown. Serve warm or at room temperature.

Makes 8 servings

Dump Cake

1 can (20 ounces) crushed pineapple with juice, undrained
1 can (21 ounces) cherry pie filling
1 package DUNCAN HINES® Moist Deluxe® Classic Yellow Cake Mix
1 cup chopped pecans or walnuts
½ cup (1 stick) butter or margarine, cut into thin slices

1. Preheat oven to 350°F. Grease 13×9-inch pan.

2. Dump pineapple with juice into prepared pan. Spread evenly. Dump in pie filling. Spread evenly. Sprinkle cake mix evenly over cherry layer. Sprinkle pecans over cake mix. Dot with butter. Bake at 350°F for 50 minutes or until top is lightly browned. Serve warm or at room temperature.

Makes 12 to 16 servings

tip:

You can use DUNCAN HINES® Moist Deluxe® Pineapple Supreme Cake Mix in place of Moist Deluxe® Yellow Cake Mix.

Dump Cake

Pineapple Upside-Down Cake

1 (8-ounce) can crushed pineapple in juice, undrained

2 tablespoons margarine, melted, divided

½ cup firmly packed light brown sugar

6 whole maraschino cherries

1½ cups all-purpose flour

2 tablespoons baking powder

¼ teaspoon salt

1 cup granulated sugar

½ cup MOTT'S® Natural Apple Sauce

1 whole egg

3 egg whites, beaten until stiff

1. Preheat oven to 375°F. Drain pineapple; reserve juice. Spray sides of 8-inch square baking pan with nonstick cooking spray.

2. Spread 1 tablespoon melted margarine evenly in bottom of prepared pan. Sprinkle with brown sugar; top with pineapple. Slice cherries in half. Arrange cherries, cut side up, so that when cake is cut, each piece will have cherry half in center.

3. In small bowl, combine flour, baking powder and salt.

4. In large bowl, combine granulated sugar, apple sauce, whole egg, remaining 1 tablespoon melted margarine and reserved pineapple juice.

5. Add flour mixture to apple sauce mixture; stir until well blended. Fold in egg whites. Gently pour batter over fruit, spreading evenly.

6. Bake 35 to 40 minutes or until lightly browned. Cool on wire rack 10 minutes. Invert cake onto serving plate. Serve warm or cool completely. Cut into 12 pieces.

Makes 12 servings

Pineapple Upside-Down Cake

Classic Pecan Pie

Prep Time: 10 minutes
Bake Time: 55 minutes

> 3 eggs
> 1 cup sugar
> 1 cup KARO® Light or Dark Corn Syrup
> 2 tablespoons margarine or butter, melted
> 1 teaspoon vanilla
> 1¼ cups pecans
> Easy-As-Pie Crust (page 234) *or* 1 (9-inch) frozen deep-dish pie crust*

*To use prepared frozen pie crust: Use 9-inch deep-dish pie crust. Do not thaw. Preheat oven and a cookie sheet. Pour filling into frozen crust. Bake on cookie sheet.

1. Preheat oven to 350°F.

2. In medium bowl with fork beat eggs slightly. Add sugar, Karo Corn Syrup, margarine and vanilla; stir until well blended. Stir in pecans. Pour into pie crust.

3. Bake 50 to 55 minutes or until knife inserted halfway between center and edge comes out clean. Cool on wire rack. *Makes 8 servings*

Almond Amaretto Pie: Substitute 1 cup sliced almonds for pecans. Add 2 tablespoons almond flavored liqueur and ½ teaspoon almond extract to filling.

Butterscotch Pecan Pie: Omit margarine; add ¼ cup heavy or whipping cream to filling.

Chocolate Chip Walnut Pie: Substitute 1 cup walnuts, coarsely chopped, for pecans. Sprinkle ½ cup semisweet chocolate chips over bottom of pie crust. Carefully pour filling into pie crust.

continued on page 234

Classic Pecan Pie

Classic Pecan Pie, continued

Easy-As-Pie Crust

Prep Time: 15 minutes

1¼ **cups flour**
⅛ **teaspoon salt**
½ **cup (1 stick) margarine or butter**
2 **tablespoons cold water**

1. In medium bowl, combine flour and salt. With pastry blender or 2 knives, cut in margarine until mixture resembles fine crumbs.

2. Sprinkle water over flour mixture while tossing with fork to blend well. Press dough firmly into ball.

3. On lightly floured surface roll out to 12-inch circle. Fit loosely into 9-inch pie plate. Trim and flute edge. Fill and bake as recipe directs.   *Makes 1 (9-inch) pie crust*

Baked Pie Shell: Preheat oven to 450°F. Pierce pie crust thoroughly with fork. Bake 10 to 15 minutes or until light brown.

Hershey's Red Velvet Cake

½ cup (1 stick) butter or margarine, softened

1½ cups sugar

2 eggs

1 teaspoon vanilla extract

1 cup buttermilk or sour milk*

2 tablespoons (1-ounce bottle) red food color

2 cups all-purpose flour

⅓ cup HERSHEY'S Cocoa

1 teaspoon salt

1½ teaspoons baking soda

1 tablespoon white vinegar

1 can (16 ounces) ready-to-spread vanilla frosting

HERSHEY'S MINI CHIPS™ Semi-Sweet Chocolate Chips or HERSHEY'S Milk Chocolate Chips (optional)

*To sour milk: Use 1 tablespoon white vinegar plus milk to equal 1 cup.

1. Heat oven to 350°F. Grease and flour 13×9×2-inch baking pan.**

2. Beat butter and sugar in large bowl; add eggs and vanilla, beating well. Stir together buttermilk and food color. Stir together flour, cocoa and salt; add alternately to butter mixture with buttermilk mixture, mixing well. Stir in baking soda and vinegar. Pour into prepared pan.

3. Bake 30 to 35 minutes or until wooden pick inserted in center comes out clean. Cool completely in pan on wire rack. Frost; garnish with chocolate chips, if desired.

Makes about 15 servings

**This recipe can be made in 2 (9-inch) cake pans. Bake at 350°F for 30 to 35 minutes.*

Double Berry Layer Cake

1 package DUNCAN HINES® Moist Deluxe® Strawberry Supreme Cake Mix
⅔ cup strawberry jam
2½ cups fresh blueberries, rinsed, drained
1 container (8 ounces) frozen whipped topping, thawed
Fresh strawberry slices for garnish

1. Preheat oven to 350°F. Grease and flour two 9-inch round cake pans.

2. Prepare, bake and cool cakes following package directions for basic recipe.

3. Place one cake layer on serving plate. Spread with ⅓ cup strawberry jam. Arrange 1 cup blueberries on jam. Spread half the whipped topping to within ½ inch of cake edge. Place second cake layer on top. Repeat with remaining ⅓ cup strawberry jam, 1 cup blueberries and remaining whipped topping. Garnish with strawberry slices and remaining ½ cup blueberries. Refrigerate until ready to serve.

Makes 12 servings

tip:

For best results, cut cake with serrated knife and clean the knife after each slice.

Double Berry Layer Cake

Carrot Layer Cake

CAKE

 1 package DUNCAN HINES® Moist Deluxe® Classic Yellow Cake Mix

 4 eggs

 ½ cup vegetable oil

 3 cups grated carrots

 1 cup finely chopped nuts

 2 teaspoons ground cinnamon

CREAM CHEESE FROSTING

 1 package (8 ounces) cream cheese, softened

 ¼ cup (½ stick) butter or margarine, softened

 2 teaspoons vanilla extract

 4 cups confectioners' sugar

1. Preheat oven to 350°F. Grease and flour two 8- or 9-inch round baking pans.

2. For cake, combine cake mix, eggs, oil, carrots, nuts and cinnamon in large bowl. Beat at low speed with electric mixer until moistened. Beat at medium speed for 2 minutes. Pour into prepared pans. Bake at 350°F for 35 to 40 minutes or until toothpick inserted into centers comes out clean. Cool.

3. For cream cheese frosting, place cream cheese, butter and vanilla extract in large bowl. Beat at low speed until smooth and creamy. Add confectioners' sugar gradually, beating until smooth. Add more sugar to thicken, or milk or water to thin frosting, as needed. Fill and frost cooled cake. Garnish with whole pecans. *Makes 12 to 16 servings*

Carrot Layer Cake

Fantasy Angel Food Cake

1 package DUNCAN HINES® Angel Food Cake Mix
Red and green food coloring
1 container DUNCAN HINES® Creamy Home-Style Cream Cheese Frosting

1. Preheat oven to 350°F.

2. Prepare cake following package directions. Divide batter into thirds and place in 3 different bowls. Add a few drops red food coloring to one. Add a few drops green food coloring to another. Stir each until well blended. Leave the third one plain. Spoon pink batter into ungreased 10-inch tube pan. Cover with white batter and top with green batter. Bake and cool following package directions.

3. To make cream cheese glaze, heat frosting in microwave at HIGH (100% power) 20 to 30 seconds. Do not overheat. Stir until smooth. Set aside ¼ cup warm glaze. Spoon remaining glaze on top and sides of cake to completely cover. Divide remaining glaze in half and place in 2 different bowls. Add a few drops red food coloring to one. Add a few drops green food coloring to the other. Stir each until well blended. Using a teaspoon, drizzle green glaze around edge of cake so it will run down sides. Repeat with pink glaze.

Makes 16 servings

tip:

For marble cake, drop batter by spoonfuls, alternating colors frequently.

Fantasy Angel Food Cake

Country Apple Rhubarb Pie

CRUST

    9-inch Classic CRISCO® Double Crust (page 244)

FILLING

    9 cups sliced peeled Granny Smith apples (about 3 pounds or 6 large apples)

  1½ cups fresh cut rhubarb (½-inch pieces), peeled if tough

    ¾ cup granulated sugar

    ½ cup firmly packed light brown sugar

    2 tablespoons PILLSBURY BEST® All-Purpose Flour

    1 tablespoon cornstarch

    1 teaspoon ground cinnamon

    ¼ teaspoon freshly grated nutmeg

GLAZE

    1 egg, beaten

    1 tablespoon water

    1 tablespoon granulated sugar

    1 teaspoon ground pecans or walnuts

    ⅛ teaspoon ground cinnamon

1. For crust, prepare as directed, using 9- or 9½-inch deep-dish pie plate. Do not bake. Heat oven to 425°F.

2. For filling, combine apples and rhubarb in large bowl. Combine ¾ cup granulated sugar, brown sugar, flour, cornstarch, 1 teaspoon cinnamon and nutmeg in medium bowl. Sprinkle over fruit. Toss to coat. Spoon into unbaked pie crust. Moisten pastry edge with water. Cover pie with lattice top, cutting strips 1¼ inches wide. Flute edge high.

3. For glaze, combine egg and water in small bowl. Brush over crust. Combine remaining glaze ingredients in small bowl. Sprinkle over crust.

continued on page 244

Country Apple Rhubarb Pie

Country Apple Rhubarb Pie, continued

4. Bake at 425°F for 20 minutes. *Reduce oven temperature to 350°F.* Bake 30 to 40 minutes or until filling in center is bubbly and crust is golden brown. *Do not overbake.* Cool to room temperature.   *Makes 1 (9- or 9½-inch) deep-dish pie (8 servings)*

9-inch Classic Crisco® Double Crust

2 cups PILLSBURY BEST® All-Purpose Flour
1 teaspoon salt
¾ CRISCO® Stick or ¾ cup CRISCO Shortening
5 tablespoons cold water

1. Spoon flour into measuring cup and level. Combine flour and salt in medium bowl.

2. Cut in CRISCO Shortening using pastry blender or 2 knives until flour is blended to form pea-size chunks.

3. Sprinkle with water, 1 tablespoon at a time. Toss lightly with fork until dough forms a ball.

4. Divide dough in half. Press half of dough between hands to form a 5- to 6-inch "pancake." Flour rolling surface and rolling pin lightly. Roll dough into circle. Trim circle 1 inch larger than upside-down pie plate. Carefully remove trimmed dough. Set aside to reroll and use for pastry cut-out garnish, if desired. Repeat with remaining half of dough.

Hot Fudge Sundae Cake

1 package DUNCAN HINES® Moist Deluxe® Dark Chocolate
Fudge Cake Mix
½ gallon brick vanilla ice cream

FUDGE SAUCE

1 can (12 ounces) evaporated milk
1¼ cups sugar
4 squares (1 ounce each) unsweetened chocolate
¼ cup (½ stick) butter or margarine
1½ teaspoons vanilla extract
¼ teaspoon salt
Whipped cream and maraschino cherries for garnish

1. Preheat oven to 350°F. Grease and flour 13×9×2-inch pan. Prepare, bake and cool cake following package directions.

2. Remove cake from pan. Split cake in half horizontally. Place bottom layer back in pan. Cut ice cream into even slices and place evenly over bottom cake layer (use all the ice cream). Place remaining cake layer over ice cream. Cover and freeze.

3. For fudge sauce, combine evaporated milk and sugar in medium saucepan. Cook, stirring constantly, over medium heat until mixture comes to a rolling boil. Boil and stir for 1 minute. Add unsweetened chocolate and stir until melted. Beat over medium heat until smooth. Remove from heat. Stir in butter, vanilla extract and salt.

4. Cut cake into squares. For each serving, place cake square on plate; spoon hot fudge sauce on top. Garnish with whipped cream and maraschino cherry.

Makes 12 to 16 servings

Tip: Fudge sauce may be prepared ahead and refrigerated in tightly sealed jar. Reheat when ready to serve.

Chocolate Almond Confection Cake

CAKE

   1 package (7 ounces) pure almond paste

   ½ cup vegetable oil, divided plus additional for greasing

   3 eggs

   1 package DUNCAN HINES® Moist Deluxe® Devil's Food Cake Mix

 1⅓ cups water

GLAZE

   1 package (6 ounces) semisweet chocolate chips

   3 tablespoons cherry jelly or seedless red raspberry jam

   2 tablespoons butter or margarine

   1 tablespoon light corn syrup

     Natural sliced almonds, for garnish

     Candied whole maraschino cherries or fresh raspberries, for garnish

1. Preheat oven to 350°F. Grease and flour 10-inch Bundt or tube pan.

2. For cake, combine almond paste and 2 tablespoons oil in large bowl. Beat at medium speed with electric mixer until blended. Add remaining oil, 2 tablespoons at a time, until blended. Add 1 egg; beat at medium speed until blended. Add remaining 2 eggs; beat until smooth. Add cake mix and water; beat at medium speed for 2 minutes. Pour into pan. Bake at 350°F for 50 to 55 minutes or until toothpick inserted in center comes out clean. Cool in pan 25 minutes. Invert onto cooling rack. Cool completely.

3. For glaze, place chocolate chips, cherry jelly, butter and corn syrup in microwave-safe medium bowl. Microwave at HIGH (100% power) for 1 to 1½ minutes. Stir until melted and smooth. Glaze top of cake. Garnish with sliced almonds and candied maraschino cherries.

Makes 12 to 16 servings

Tip: This recipe may also be prepared in the food processor. Place almond paste in work bowl with knife blade. Process until finely chopped. Add cake mix, eggs, water and oil. Process for 1 minute or until smooth. Bake and cool as directed above.

Chocolate Almond Confection Cake

Old-Fashioned Pumpkin Pie

1 cup sugar

1 tablespoon all-purpose flour

1 tablespoon WATKINS® Pumpkin Pie Spice

½ teaspoon salt

3 eggs

1½ cups mashed, cooked pumpkin or canned pumpkin

1 cup evaporated milk

1 unbaked 9-inch pie crust

Preheat oven to 400°F. Combine sugar, flour, pumpkin pie spice and salt in large bowl; beat in eggs until well blended. Stir in pumpkin and milk until smooth. Pour into pie crust. Bake for 50 minutes or until knife inserted into center comes out clean. *Makes 10 servings*

Sour Cream Pound Cake

3 cups sugar

1 cup (2 sticks) butter, softened

1 teaspoon *each* vanilla and lemon extract

6 eggs

3 cups cake flour

¼ teaspoon baking soda

1 cup dairy sour cream

Heat oven to 325°F. Butter and flour 10-inch tube pan. In large bowl, beat sugar and butter until light and fluffy. Add vanilla and lemon extract; mix well. Add eggs, one at a time, beating well after each addition. In medium bowl, combine flour and baking soda. Add to butter mixture alternately with sour cream, beating well after each addition. Pour batter into prepared pan. Bake 1 hour and 20 minutes or until toothpick inserted near center comes out clean. Cool in pan 15 minutes; invert onto wire rack and cool completely. Store tightly covered. *Makes 12 to 16 servings*

Favorite recipe from **Southeast United Dairy Industry Association, Inc.**

Old-Fashioned Pumpkin Pie

Acknowledgments

The publisher would like to thank the companies and organizations listed below for the use of their recipes and photographs in this publication.

ACH Food Companies, Inc.

Alouette® Cheese, Chavrie® Cheese, Saladena®

BelGioioso® Cheese, Inc.

Birds Eye Foods

Bob Evans®

Cherry Marketing Institute

COLLEGE INN® Broth

Crisco is a registered trademark of The J.M. Smucker Company

Del Monte Corporation

Dole Food Company, Inc.

Domino® Foods, Inc.

Duncan Hines® and Moist Deluxe® are registered trademarks of Pinnacle Foods Corp.

EAGLE BRAND®

Equal® sweetener

Filippo Berio® Olive Oil

Florida Tomato Committee

The Golden Grain Company®

Guiltless Gourmet®

Heinz North America

The Hershey Company

The Hidden Valley® Food Products Company

Hillshire Farm®

Kahlúa® Liqueur

Keebler® Company

The Kingsford® Products Co.

Lawry's® Foods

© Mars, Incorporated 2006

MASTERFOODS USA

McIlhenny Company (TABASCO® brand Pepper Sauce)

Mott's® is a registered trademark of Mott's, LLP

National Honey Board

National Onion Association

National Pork Board

National Turkey Federation

Nestlé USA

North Dakota Wheat Commission

Ortega®, A Division of B&G Foods, Inc.

The Quaker® Oatmeal Kitchens

Reckitt Benckiser Inc.

RED STAR® Yeast, a product of Lasaffre Yeast Corporation

Riviana Foods Inc.

Sargento® Foods Inc.

Smucker's® trademark of The J.M. Smucker Company

Southeast United Dairy Industry Association, Inc.

SPLENDA® is a trademark of McNeil Nutritionals, LLC

The Sugar Association, Inc.

Reprinted with permission of Sunkist Growers, Inc. All Rights Reserved.

Unilever Foods North America

Washington Apple Commission

Watkins Incorporated

Wisconsin Milk Marketing Board

METRIC CONVERSION CHART

VOLUME MEASUREMENTS (dry)

⅛ teaspoon = 0.5 mL
¼ teaspoon = 1 mL
½ teaspoon = 2 mL
¾ teaspoon = 4 mL
1 teaspoon = 5 mL
1 tablespoon = 15 mL
2 tablespoons = 30 mL
¼ cup = 60 mL
⅓ cup = 75 mL
½ cup = 125 mL
⅔ cup = 150 mL
¾ cup = 175 mL
1 cup = 250 mL
2 cups = 1 pint = 500 mL
3 cups = 750 mL
4 cups = 1 quart = 1 L

VOLUME MEASUREMENTS (fluid)

1 fluid ounce (2 tablespoons) = 30 mL
4 fluid ounces (½ cup) = 125 mL
8 fluid ounces (1 cup) = 250 mL
12 fluid ounces (1½ cups) = 375 mL
16 fluid ounces (2 cups) = 500 mL

WEIGHTS (mass)

½ ounce = 15 g
1 ounce = 30 g
3 ounces = 90 g
4 ounces = 120 g
8 ounces = 225 g
10 ounces = 285 g
12 ounces = 360 g
16 ounces = 1 pound = 450 g

DIMENSIONS

1/16 inch = 2 mm
⅛ inch = 3 mm
¼ inch = 6 mm
½ inch = 1.5 cm
¾ inch = 2 cm
1 inch = 2.5 cm

OVEN TEMPERATURES

250°F = 120°C
275°F = 140°C
300°F = 150°C
325°F = 160°C
350°F = 180°C
375°F = 190°C
400°F = 200°C
425°F = 220°C
450°F = 230°C

BAKING PAN SIZES

Utensil	Size in Inches/Quarts	Metric Volume	Size in Centimeters
Baking or Cake Pan (square or rectangular)	8×8×2	2 L	20×20×5
	9×9×2	2.5 L	23×23×5
	12×8×2	3 L	30×20×5
	13×9×2	3.5 L	33×23×5
Loaf Pan	8×4×3	1.5 L	20×10×7
	9×5×3	2 L	23×13×7
Round Layer Cake Pan	8×1½	1.2 L	20×4
	9×1½	1.5 L	23×4
Pie Plate	8×1¼	750 mL	20×3
	9×1¼	1 L	23×3
Baking Dish or Casserole	1 quart	1 L	—
	1½ quart	1.5 L	—
	2 quart	2 L	—